The World Book of Space Exploration

WONDERS

OF THE

UNIVERSE

The World Book of Space Exploration

WONDERS OF THE

UNIVERSE

Published by
World Book, Inc.
a Scott Fetzer company
Chicago

Staff

Publisher
William H. Nault

Editorial

Editor in chief
Robert O. Zeleny

Executive editor
Dominic J. Miccolis

Associate editor
Scott Thomas

Contributing editor
Waldemar Bojczuk

Permissions editor
Janet T. Peterson

Art

Art director
Roberta Dimmer

Assistant art director
Joe Gound

Photography director
John S. Marshall

Photographs editor
Barbara Bennett

Production coordinator
Kelly M. Shea

Book design
Chestnut House

Product production

Executive director
Peter Mollman

Director, manufacturing
Henry Koval

Manager, manufacturing
Sandra Van den Broucke

Director, pre-press services
Jerry Stack

Product managers
Randi Park
Joann Seastrom

Proofreaders
Anne Dillon
Marguerite Hoye
Esther Johns
Daniel J. Marotta

Contents

THE SKY ABOVE, THE EARTH BELOW

This Mesopotamian boundary stone of 1100 B.C. shows the moon at the top between its "children"—Venus (left) and the sun (right).

Lightning splits the night sky over Kitt Peak National Observatory in Arizona.

Since the dawn of the human race, the night sky has been the object of much study and speculation. Persons from all walks of life have tried to explain the wonders that appear night after night in the sky. This section reviews some of the major theories that have attempted to explain our place in the universe. It also introduces some of the important stargazers who made major discoveries about the sky above and the earth below.

A portion of the Bayeux Tapestry, created in France in the Middle Ages, shows King Harold of England being told of a bright comet in 1066.

ISTI MIRANT STELLA

HAROLD

THE NIGHT SKY

Go out on a clear, moonless night into the country, far from the air pollution and lights of any city or town, lie down on the ground, and look up. The sight is overwhelming. Stars by the hundreds fill the heavens. Some brilliant and some faint, they dot the black sky from one horizon to the other.

Most of us don't see the night sky in its true splendor, because we live in places where artificial lights illuminate the sky and spoil the view. But from a truly dark, rural location, our view of the heavens is essentially the same that every age of the human race has beheld. Stone Age men and women looked up at this sight from their campfires. Shepherds in ancient Mesopotamia and Egypt marveled at the same celestial view we see today.

The ancient monument of Stonehenge in England was built sometime between 2800 and 2000 B.C. It may have served as an astronomical calendar to predict the seasons of the year and even eclipses of the sun and moon.

Today, we know this impression is completely wrong. Earth is round, not flat. It is a tiny speck adrift in a universe so huge that no one can imagine its size. The stars are huge balls of glowing gas—trillions and trillions of them, unbelievably far away. Many of them probably have planets of their own. Space is full of other wonders so strange, so bizarre, so beautiful and unimaginable that no one could possibly have dreamed them up before they were discovered.

But what we know about the universe has taken ages of slow detective work. There were many false starts, wrong turns— and a few cowardly retreats.

ANCIENT IDEAS

The earliest peoples thought, naturally enough, that the universe was only what they saw: a sky dome over a flat Earth. Beyond that, they simply made up stories. The ancient Babylonians believed the world floated on an immense ocean, while the gods lived on top of the sky dome. The sun came through a door in the sky every morning and left through another door in the evening.

What are the stars? How big is the universe? Where do we fit in? People have been asking these questions since earliest times, but the answers have been slow in coming.

At first, people could judge only from what they saw: a great black dome of sky arching above a flat Earth, like a bowl turned upside down on a tabletop, with the people inside the bowl. This is still the way the universe looks: simple, small, self-contained.

11

The Egyptians saw the universe as a room, with the sky as the ceiling and Earth as the floor. Egypt, of course, was in the center. The stars hung from the sky-ceiling like lamps, and the sun god Ra sailed around the sky once a day in a boat.

As the ancient Hindus imagined it, the flat Earth rested on the backs of four elephants, who were standing on the back of a giant turtle, which swam in a river of milk.

Such ideas must have seemed perfectly logical to the people who believed them. They would have scoffed at the notion that Earth is round and moves through space. But there was one big difference between their ideas and those that would follow. Their myths were not based on any evidence. They were simply made up. The idea of testing such ideas to see whether or not they are true never seems to have occurred to the people of ancient Mesopotamia and Egypt.

The ancient astronomer-priests did know much practical astronomy. They could forecast eclipses and tell just what time

Many ancient cultures worshiped the sun. Here, the Egyptian pharaoh Akhenaton, who ruled Egypt from about 1367 to 1350 B.C., is shown worshiping the sun god, Aton.

12

of year certain stars would appear at dawn. But they did not understand the reasons for the things they observed in the sky. They thought of the celestial bodies as gods, or as whimsical, chaotic forces that no one could understand. So there seemed to be no point in trying to find out why these bodies behaved as they did.

GREECE AND THE BIRTH OF SCIENCE

About 2,500 years ago, in the land of Greece, a new way of thinking began to take root. In the broadest terms, it was the idea that the world is knowable—that the universe acts in predictable ways according to natural laws.

The Greek philosophers developed and refined geometry and much of mathematics, and they were amazed to discover the hidden laws that numbers obey. Pythagoras believed that the secret laws of numbers were so holy and perfect they should be kept hidden from ordinary people. One of Pythagoras' beliefs was that Earth was round. Other philosophers, studying the motions of the heavenly bodies, proposed various ideas for why the sun, moon, stars, and planets move as they do in the sky. They applied their mathematics to the problem, and some came to believe that the celestial bodies are carried around the sky on invisible, hollow spheres, with Earth at the center.

This might not seem like much improvement on sun boats, elephants, and turtles. But there was a big difference. The Greeks' universe was not run by the whims of irrational gods; it was orderly like a piece of machinery. Its motions could be studied and predicted.

The first person to accurately measure the size of Earth was a scholar named Eratosthenes who lived in the Egyptian city of Alexandria, then part of the Greek Empire. He knew that in the city of Syene, farther south, the sun stood straight overhead at noon on the day of the summer solstice, so that pillars cast no shadows and sunlight shone to the bottoms of wells. But on the same day in Alexandria, the sun was not quite overhead, and a vertical post cast a shadow. Measurement showed that here, the sunlight fell at an angle of about 7° from the vertical—or about one-fiftieth of a circle. Believing in the round-earth theory proposed by Pythagoras, Eratosthenes set out to determine the size of Earth.

He hired a man to pace out the distance between the two cities. It came to about 500

Claudius Ptolemaeus, better known as Ptolemy, was one of the greatest astronomers and geographers of ancient times. He made his astronomical observations at Alexandria, Egypt, about A.D. 150.

This colored woodcut from the 1500's shows the Ptolemaic universe, with Earth in the center, and the sun, moon, and other planets revolving around it.

miles (800 kilometers). Since he knew this distance had to be one-fiftieth of Earth's circumference, then Earth must be about 25,000 miles (40,000 kilometers) around.

14   He was right. Simply by measuring the angle formed by shadows, he had calculated the size of Earth.

For anyone interested in the mysteries of nature, this was an exciting time to be alive. Other philosophers realized Earth is not motionless but rotates, or turns on its axis, once a day; this is why the sun, moon, and stars appear to rise and set. When we see the sun go down in the west, we are actually seeing the western horizon rise. The rising and setting is not due to any motion of the sun.

Aristarchus, another Greek, went further. Knowing the size and shape of Earth, he managed to estimate the distance to the moon. By studying the phases of the moon, he deduced that the sun is much farther away, which

meant it had to be bigger than Earth. He then proposed that the planets—"wandering stars" seen among the constellations—circle the sun. He declared that Earth itself is a planet and does the same.

He got it entirely right. Human thought had gone from a flat Earth and dome sky to the correct picture of our spinning planet flying through space—and all about 1,900 years before the invention of the telescope.

Most other thinkers of the time rejected Aristarchus' idea as too strange to be true. But the evidence was there. In time all would probably have come to believe it. Many other discoveries were being made in other areas of science—geography, physics, medicine, mathematics. There is no telling where it all might have led. But ancient Greek science had a fatal flaw. For the most part, the philosophers did not believe in getting involved with the practical world. They believed science and mathematics were too pure and holy to be taught to common people. But the people who built things— who did the work and could have put new discoveries to use—*were* the common people. So, much of Greek science was stillborn. It died out in the wars, tyranny, and chaos that finally destroyed classical civilization. In the centuries that followed, the discoveries of the Greeks were all but forgotten.

One idea of the Greeks, though, did arouse interest during the Middle Ages. Plato and Aristotle taught that all was divided into two parts: the pure, perfect, and eternal celestial regions above, and the dirty, flawed, changing Earth below. This division of sky from Earth seemed to match Christian teachings about divisions between perfect heaven versus fallen humanity, pure soul versus impure body. So the ideas of Aristotle were widely discussed

and were accepted by many scholars. But church leaders put an end to inquiry into what astronomical bodies really are. The flat Earth returned, and for a long time it was even forbidden to teach that Earth is round.

THE COPERNICAN REVOLUTION

Astronomy did not stop during this time, however. There was much interest in predicting where the planets would be among the constellations on any given day. The best system for doing this was a mathematical description of the paths along which the sun, the moon, and each of the planets were supposed to orbit the Earth, developed around A.D. 150 by an Egyptian astronomer named Ptolemy.

When some people in the late Middle Ages tried to picture the

15

solar system as Ptolemy described it, they imagined that an arrangement of invisible crystal spheres carried the celestial bodies through the sky. They believed that the moon, for example, was attached to a small, turning sphere, which in turn rode upon a large, rotating sphere that encircled the Earth. The sun and each of the planets also traveled through the heavens on its own set of rotating crystal spheres. Beyond the spheres of the planets was one that carried the stars. Earth was just off the center of the series of spheres that surrounded it. This system was complicated and awkward, but it worked fairly well as a mathematical tool for solving the motions of the planets.

However, during the mid- to late Middle Ages, some men who carefully observed the planets found that the Ptolemaic system did not work perfectly. And some people had a hard time believing the sky was really jammed full of invisible machinery. Eventually, a few even began to suggest that a way should be found to describe the motions of the planets more ac-

curately. One such person was Nicolaus Copernicus, who lived during the early 1500's. Copernicus was a canon of the Roman Catholic Church in what is now Poland. He spent much of his life trying to find a more philosophically and aesthetically satisfactory way than Ptolemy's theory to account for the motions of the planets. He succeeded—by assuming that the planets, including Earth, travel around the sun. The great theory of Aristarchus had been rediscovered.

Copernicus was a timid, reclusive man. He did not publish his theory until shortly before his death. Although Copernicus' theory received little attention at first, it eventually raised stormy debates. This was because many traditional academics and clergy believed deeply in a motionless Earth at the center of the universe, and in Aristotle's perfect, invisible spheres filling the skies with perfect circular motion.

A lively participant in those debates was Galileo Galilei, an outspoken and popular teacher of mathematics in Italy. In 1609, Galileo first looked at the sky with the newly invented telescope. With it, he saw that the moon has mountains and plains like those on Earth—though followers of Aristotle taught that the moon was a smooth, perfect sphere. He discovered four tiny moons orbiting the planet Jupiter—though traditionalists who believed in perfection in the heavens denied that such things could exist. Some even refused to look. He discovered that the planet Venus shows phases like those of the moon, which he saw as evidence that Venus circles the sun.

For such reasons, Galileo became a champion of the Copernican theory. He was a sharp-tongued debater and made many enemies. Some of them went to church authorities and urged

16

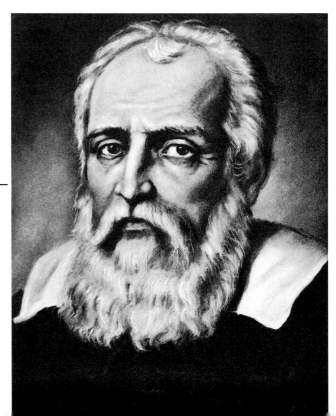

Galileo Galilei (1564–1642) has been called by some historians the founder of modern experimental science. Among other innovations, he made the first practical use of the telescope to discover many new facts about the moon and planets.

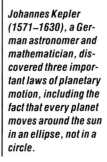

Johannes Kepler (1571–1630), a German astronomer and mathematician, discovered three important laws of planetary motion, including the fact that every planet moves around the sun in an ellipse, not in a circle.

Two of Galileo's telescopes are on display in the Museum of the History of Science in Florence, Italy.

that Galileo be silenced, on the grounds that a moving Earth contradicts the Bible. It was a deadly accusation to make. A few years before, the Catholic Inquisition had sentenced Giordano Bruno, a Dominican priest and freethinker, to be burned alive at the stake, partly for teaching the Copernican theory.

The officials of the Inquisition summoned Galileo. They ordered him to abandon the "absurd and heretical" notion that the sun is stationary and Earth moves around it. Galileo agreed not to teach the Copernican theory as being true. A few years later, however, he published a book that clearly defended it. He was summoned back to the Inquisition and forced, under threat of torture, to deny formally and publicly that Earth goes around the sun. For the rest of his life, he was kept under house arrest, constantly guarded and watched.

But the Copernican theory could not be suppressed. It explained the behavior of the planets too well. And it did away with some of the imaginary celestial clockwork of Ptolemy.

Tycho Brahe, a Danish nobleman, spent many years observing the positions of planets and measuring planetary positions in relation to Earth and the sun. These measurements were far more accurate than any that had been recorded before. Using Brahe's data, Johannes Kepler, a teacher in Germany, greatly improved the Copernican system. After years of wrestling with the mathematics, he figured out that Earth and the planets move around the sun not in circles, but in ellipses, or oval-shaped paths. Kepler also discovered two mathematical principles that describe the speed of the planets in their orbits. With Kepler's three laws of planetary motion, the shape and speed of the planetary orbits were at last understood.

In the process, our true place in the solar system had been revealed. We are not at the center; rather, we are on a relatively small planet that revolves around the sun.

EARTH AND SKY REUNITED

The story is told that Isaac Newton, an English scientist, was sitting under an apple tree. An apple fell to the ground, and he suddenly realized that the force that pulls the apple to Earth also holds the moon in or-

Danish astronomer Tycho Brahe (1546–1601) developed a systematic approach for observing the planets and stars. He is pictured here in an observatory he built on the Danish island of Ven.

EFFIGIES TYCHONIS BRAHE O. F.
ÆDIFICII ET INSTRUMENTORVM
ASTRONOMICORVM STRVCTORIS
A.º DOMINI 1587 ÆTATIS SVÆ 40

18

bit. But, he wondered, what laws
govern the effect of gravity?
How does gravity work?

Newton searched for an explanation for years, and his solution
was his great law of gravitation,
a very simple but far-reaching
notion: every object pulls every
other object toward it by a gravitational force. The more massive
an object, the stronger its gravity; the farther away it is, the
weaker is gravity's effect. Earth
is by far the most massive object
near us, so it exerts the strongest
force on us.

The moon is indeed subject to
Earth's gravity, but instead of
falling down, Newton showed, it
must circle Earth in an orbit. It
is, in effect, falling around Earth.

To picture how an orbit
works, imagine a marble on the
side of a bowl. If you simply let
it go, gravity pulls it straight to
the center. But if you flip it sideways, it circles around the center without falling in. The force
pulling toward the center is bal-
anced by the marble's sideways
momentum. In the same way,
the moon circles Earth, and the

*This large telescope
was constructed in the
seventeenth century
by the Polish astrono-
mer and instrument
maker Johannes He-
velius. He built the
world's leading ob-
servatory in Gdańsk,
Poland. It was de-
stroyed by fire in
1679.*

Sir Isaac Newton (1642–1727), an English scientist, astronomer, and mathematician, showed through his theory of gravitation how the universe is held together.

This huge reflecting telescope, nicknamed the "Leviathan," was built in 1845 by Lord Rosse, an Irish astronomer. It had a 72-inch (180-centimeter) mirror made of metal.

planets circle the sun. The marble in the bowl will eventually slow down and stop because of friction, but there is almost no friction in space. So the moon and planets keep circling forever.

When Newton applied his mathematical formula of gravity to the planets, he found that it almost exactly accounted for the planets' motions and the elliptical shapes of their orbits. All the workings of the solar system were explained by the same, simple law that governs a falling stone here on Earth.

Thus, Newton not only laid the foundations for much of modern physics, he overturned the doctrine of Aristotle that celestial bodies are some different, more ideal order of being than things on Earth. The objects in the sky have the same physical nature and obey the same physical law as things on the ground. Or, to look at it another way, we ourselves are made of celestial material. Our ordinary, everyday world is part of the cosmos. The celestial regions were once again fully open to inquiry and discovery.

THE GROWTH OF MODERN ASTRONOMY

By the time Newton died in 1727, astronomy and many other sciences were making great advances in Europe. Each new discovery became the foundation from which others could be made. Newton himself said that if he saw farther than anyone had before, it was because he stood on the shoulders of giants. His own work became the base for other astronomers to stand on and see farther still.

In all the time the planets had been studied, the stars were little more than background scenery. They were clearly farther away than the planets, but not much else could be told about them. Once Earth was known to go around the sun, however, a method for finding their distance became available.

The motion of Earth from one side of its orbit to the other should make nearby stars seem to move back and forth with respect to farther ones. You can

Bigger and better telescopes are constantly being pointed toward the sky. This large optical telescope is located at Kitt Peak National Observatory in Arizona.

Three basic types of telescopes

A refracting telescope
is a tube with lenses
at each end. Light en-
ters the telescope
through the objective
lens. This lens re-
fracts, or bends, the
light toward the eye-
piece lens.

A reflecting telescope
uses a curved mirror
as its objective. The
mirror gathers light
and focuses it on a flat
mirror suspended in
the center of the tele-
scope tube. The flat
mirror reflects the
light to the eyepiece
lens.

see this effect, known as parallax, by moving your head from side to side; near objects seem to move back and forth with respect to more distant scenery. Try it. The nearer something is, the larger its apparent motion.

Not until the early 1800's were telescopes accurate enough to measure the tiny parallax motion of stars. Among the first to detect this motion was Friedrich Wilhelm Bessel. He determined that the star 61 Cygni is about 65 trillion miles (105 trillion kilometers) away, or some 700,000 times farther than the sun.

At such great distances, stars would have to be extremely bright for us to see them at all. In fact, they would have to be just about as luminous as the sun itself. The idea that stars are suns was not new—but now scientists had a way to determine more precisely the brightness of

each star. The known universe became unimaginably larger.

And once again, our place turned out to be on the sidelines. The sun is not the center of the universe, but only a very ordinary star lost among swarms of stars scattered throughout space.

Meanwhile, better and better telescopes were being turned to the sky, and hundreds of new techniques were invented to analyze the size, temperature, distance, motion, and chemical composition of the stars. Double stars were discovered—pairs of stars orbiting around each other. Star clusters—nests of less than a dozen to many thousands of stars—were revealed, as were nebulae, strange objects like great luminous clouds in space. The planets were scrutinized with intense care; and each yielded secrets about what kind of world it was.

As our view enlarged ever farther, it became clear that all the stars we see are part of one vast assemblage, now called the Milky Way galaxy, of which we are a part. The Milky Way contains more than 100 billion stars. And once again, not even the Milky Way turned out to be central. At unbelievably greater distances, whole other galaxies were discovered—hundreds more at first, then thousands more, then millions.

In recent decades, astronomy has expanded faster and faster. Astronomers now study not just the visible light of the universe, but its infrared and ultraviolet light, radio emissions, X rays, and gamma rays.

And, after thousands of years of looking up in longing, we have begun to travel into space ourselves. For the first time, we are learning about other worlds by actually going there. The rest of this book is a survey of some of the amazing things we have discovered about the wonders of the universe.

23

A radio telescope collects and measures faint radio waves given off by objects in space. The waves are collected in the reflector dish, focused onto the receiver, and deflected into the vertex box. The waves are converted into electronic signals and are sent to the computer, which transcribes them into a graph showing the signal strength of the waves.

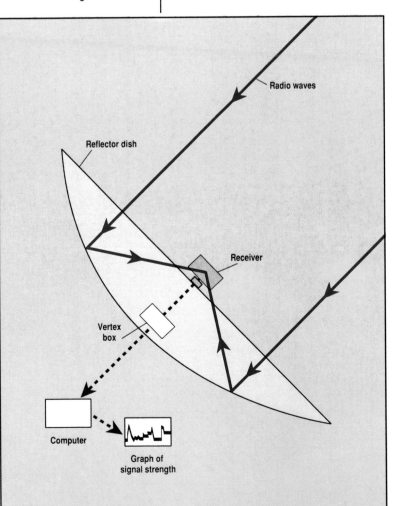

Radio waves

Reflector dish

Receiver

Vertex box

Computer

Graph of signal strength

THE REALM OF THE SUN

The sun is the center of our part of the universe. It is the main source of energy and the sustainer of life. Traveling around it are many interesting and unusual objects, including planets, asteroids, and comets. These objects each have their own unique features—from a volcano three times the height of Mount Everest, to a canyon that would stretch the length of the United States, to an entire world made of ice and smooth as a billiard ball.

The sun, planets, moons, and other objects that we call the solar system are the subject of this section. They are truly a realm of the fantastic.

On the right is a photograph of Earth as seen from space. On the far right is the crater Yuty on Mars, as photographed by the Viking 1 space probe.

This picture of the solar corona was photographed in Bolivia during an eclipse of the sun on November 12, 1966.

In this color-coded image of Comet West, each color corresponds to a different level of light intensity.

The Voyager 2 space probe took this photograph of Saturn and its rings.

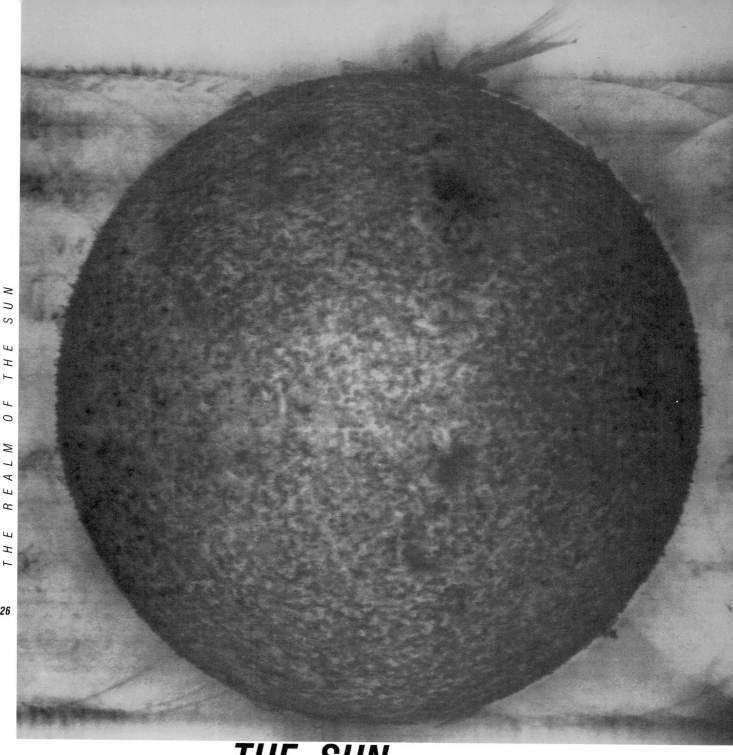

THE SUN

We live our lives under the influence of a glowing ball of gas, whose energy lights our days, gives us life-sustaining warmth, and nourishes all living things. The star we call the sun is an average star as stars go, just approaching middle age in its 10-billion-year life span. But to us, it is the most important star in the universe. It is also the nearest, and for that reason, the one that we know the most about.

From Earth, the sun is a brilliant yellow-white disk, too bright to look at. Yet it is some 93 million miles (158 million kilometers) away, so far that its light takes more than 8 minutes and 20 seconds to reach us.

From here the sun looks small, but it is actually about 865,000 miles (1,384,000 kilometers) across. Like most stars, it is made mostly of hydrogen (about 75 percent of the sun's mass), with a smaller amount of helium (about 24 percent), and much smaller quantities of oxygen, carbon, nitrogen, and other elements.

THE SUN'S NUCLEAR FIRES

The sun produces an incredible amount of energy. About 30 minutes worth of the radiation Earth receives from the sun is enough to equal all the energy produced by every city and town on Earth in a year; and yet we receive only one two-billionths of the sun's total energy output. What could produce such enormous quantities of energy? The answer is nuclear fusion, the same process responsible for the awesome destructive power of a hydrogen bomb.

The sun's energy is unleashed deep within its interior, in its core. There, hydrogen atoms collide and fuse together to form helium atoms, and this fusion process produces the sun's energy. Because the core is hidden beneath other layers of gas thousands of miles thick, astronomers cannot directly observe it. But with the aid of sophisticated instruments and computers, they can calculate what it must be like. It is certainly extremely hot—probably 27,000,000° F. (15,000,000° C). The gas in the core is so highly compressed by the weight of the overlying layers that it is estimated to be 15 times more dense than lead—hardly like a gas at all.

If it were not so hot, the sun would surely collapse under its own gravity. But the extreme heat within the sun creates very high pressures that push outward, counteracting gravity.

The intense energy produced by nuclear fusion in the sun's core travels outward into the surrounding gas. Through most of the sun, energy travels by radiation—the same process that makes your face feel warm when you look through the window of a hot oven.

But in the upper layers, the energy travels by convection, the same process by which hot water in a tub cools off. In the sun's convection zone, gas heats up until it expands to form bubbles called granules. Because these are less dense—and therefore lighter—than their surroundings, the granules rise toward the sun's surface layers until they reach a layer called the photosphere, where they radiate energy, cool off, and sink back into deeper layers again.

The energy carried up by the granules is released in the photosphere in the form of sunlight. Although it contains all the colors of the rainbow, sunlight is predominantly yellow. Scientists know that the color of a star depends on its temperature. The photosphere's yellow color corresponds to a temperature of about 10,000° F. (5,500° C).

The sun is an enormous ball of extremely hot gases. Energy is produced by means of thermonuclear reactions in the core. It flows into the radiative zone and on through the violently turbulent convection zone. It then enters the photosphere and continues on through the rest of the sun's atmosphere, eventually flowing into space as radiant heat and light.

Convection zone —————————

Radiative zone —————————

28

Core —————

Photosphere —————————

THE SUN'S SURFACE

The photosphere is the visible surface layer of the sun. It is not, of course, a solid surface. It is a thin layer, only about 340 miles (544 kilometers) thick. On astronomers' photographs, the photosphere has a coarse, grainy appearance resembling boiling oatmeal. And in fact, the grains are really the tops of the granules rising from the interior of the sun. Astronomers call this texture granulation.

Above the photosphere is a sparse, transparent layer called the chromosphere. It can be seen by the eye only during a total eclipse of the sun. Then it forms a thin, flame-red ring around the black shadow of the moon. The chromosphere is much hotter than the photosphere below, reaching temperatures of 50,000° F. (27,800° C) or more in its tenuous upper reaches.

Beyond the chromosphere is the corona, where temperatures reach some 4,000,000° F. (2,200,000° C). This jump in temperature between the chromosphere and corona occurs in a transition region only a few tens of miles (kilometers) across.

The corona is the outermost layer of the sun's atmosphere, stretching millions of miles (kilometers) into space. During a total solar eclipse, the corona may look like the petals of a pale white flower surrounding the blackened sun and the fiery red chromosphere.

SUNSPOTS AND THE SOLAR CYCLE

The photosphere is often dotted with markings called sunspots. Sunspots look dark compared to the bright photosphere because they are some 4,000° F. (2,200° C) cooler, yet they are still as hot as an acetylene torch. A typical sunspot might be 6,000 miles (10,000 kilometers) across—almost large enough to swallow Earth. But sunspots five

times that size have also been recorded.

Sunspots show that the sun, like Earth, rotates. Photographs taken hours or days apart show sunspots moving across the solar disk. It takes about 25 earth-days for the sun's equator to make one full rotation, but the sun's poles are slower: they take 35 or 36 earth-days to go around. In this way, gaseous bodies like the sun are different from solid bodies, such as Earth, all parts of which rotate at the same rate at all latitudes.

The number of sunspots visible on the sun varies. When many sunspots are present, the sun is active; when there are few sunspots, the sun is relatively quiet. Astronomers have found that every 11 years the number of sunspots reaches a maximum. These sunspot maxima are the times when the sun is at its peak of activity. Roughly five and one-half years after each sunspot maximum, there is a sunspot minimum, and the sun is at its least active. Then, five and one-half years after that, another maximum occurs. The whole 11-year progression is called the sunspot cycle.

Some scientists have found evidence that climate on Earth may be influenced by the solar cycle. During most of the 1600's, for example, there were far fewer sunspots on the sun than usual. Some astronomers believe this may have been the reason for the unusually cold weather that persisted during those years.

What keeps sunspots cool? Scientists don't know for sure. But one possible answer is that convection of heat from the interior does not occur within sunspots. Instead of bubbling up and

The McMath Solar Telescope at Kitt Peak National Observatory in Arizona, the world's largest solar telescope, is operated by the National Solar Observatory.

turning over, gas within a sunspot is trapped by the sun's strong magnetic field. Solar gas is so hot that the gas molecules bang into each other with enough force to strip away the outer electrons surrounding individual atoms. Such ionized gas cannot move wherever it wants, but rather only along magnetic field lines.

SOLAR PROMINENCES

Observations of the edge of the sun, using special filters, show flamelike clouds of glowing gas extending up into the sun's corona. These clouds, which are called prominences, can linger for periods from a few hours to days. Though prominences are most easily observed at the edge of the sun, they can occur anywhere on the surface. Sometimes a prominence will erupt away from the sun in a spectacular blast.

OUTBURSTS FROM THE SUN

The sun's steady shining is accompanied by other violent bursts of activity. On occasion, a brilliant outburst called a flare erupts in the chromosphere. A major flare can explode with the power of a 2 billion megaton bomb. When radiation from the flare reaches Earth eight minutes later, it can play havoc with radio transmissions. Protons and

This cutaway view of the McMath Solar Telescope on Kitt Peak shows how it works. Sunlight striking Mirror A is reflected down the diagonal shaft. Mirror B, an image-forming mirror, sends the light back up the shaft. Mirror C finally reflects the image onto a table for observation.

Sun rays

Mirror A

Reflected beam

Mirror C

Table for observation

Ground

Spectrograph shaft

Mirror B

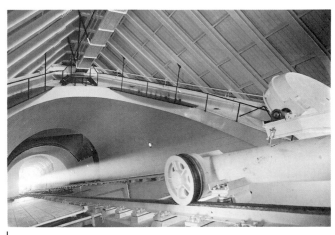

This is a view of the light path within the inclined tunnel of the McMath Solar Telescope.

electrons spewed out by the flare reach Earth in about 36 hours and may enter our upper atmosphere, where they create an aurora. For astronauts in space, the radiation from a large flare is a great hazard.

Flares are most common during times of sunspot maximum. Scientists are still trying to find out why flares occur and how their enormous energy is released. Current theories suggest that flares make use of energy stored in the sun's magnetic field.

32

Shown in its early stages, the largest solar prominence ever observed became almost as large as the sun itself within one hour. After a few hours, it had disappeared completely.

The aurora borealis, or northern lights, is a natural display of light, caused by the interaction of the solar wind with Earth's upper atmosphere.

The sun's corona evaporates away in a stream of charged particles called the solar wind. The solar wind pervades the solar system to its very edge, where it merges with winds from other stars.

THE DEATH OF THE SUN

Like all stars, the sun will not last forever. The sun is burning its hydrogen at a rate of 11 billion pounds (5 billion kilograms) per second. But even at that rate, it has several billion years left before nearly all of the hydrogen in its core is converted into helium. Astronomers believe that as it uses up hydrogen, the sun will grow in size and brightness. Five and one-half billion years from now, the sun may be 1.4 times its present size and about twice its present brightness. All the hydrogen in the core will be gone; only the helium "ashes" of its nuclear fires will remain.

At this point, not enough energy will be produced in the sun's core to counteract the star's own gravity. As the fires in the core die out, the core will begin to contract. But the collapse will generate enough heat to burn the thin shell of leftover hydrogen around the core. This new fire will cause the star's surface layers to expand. Astronomers calculate that after an additional 1.5 billion years, the sun will be 3.3 times larger than it is today, and 250 million years after that, it will swell to 100 times its present size—all the way out to the innermost planet, Mercury. It could be 500 times brighter than it is today, what astronomers call a red giant. The intense heat from the enormous, deep-red sun will turn Earth's surface into a sea of molten rock.

After a brief but fiery career as a red giant (lasting perhaps 250 million years), the sun will contract again as the very last of its hydrogen is converted to helium. Temperatures in the core will rise as the sun falls in on itself, and when the core heats to 180,000,000° F. (100,000,000° C), a new type of nuclear fusion will occur, in which helium atoms combine to produce carbon.

When the sun's helium "ashes" finally ignite, a tremendous explosion will probably blow away much of the sun's outer layers. In time, fierce solar winds will blow all but the core itself into space. All that will be left of our star will be a hot, dense remnant called a white dwarf, about the same size as Earth and perhaps one-thousandth as bright as the sun today.

During billions of years as a white dwarf—astronomers can't say how long with any certainty—the sun will continually cool down, and it will eventually become a cold, dark ember of the glorious beacon it is today.

THE SOLAR SYSTEM

On our tour of the realm of the sun, we will explore the various worlds that make up the solar system. Giant worlds made of gas and ice, rocky worlds scorched by the sun, and cratered worlds with barely a smooth patch of ground all exist within the same system of planets and moons. And, of course, so does Earth—a planet unlike any other.

It seems almost unbelievable that such varied worlds can exist in the same solar system. Even planetary scientists and astronomers are often amazed by new discoveries, such as giant volcanoes and canyons on Mars, active volcanoes on Jupiter's moon Io, and a nitrogen ocean on Neptune's satellite Triton.

The story of how these worlds formed is hidden from us, and we must be clever detectives to find out the details of their early history. After 20 years of intensive exploration of the sun and planets, both from Earth and with spacecraft, the details are still mostly unknown. But researchers have pieced together a rough outline of the formation of the solar system.

A BEGINNING IN DARKNESS

About 4.6 billion years ago, a vast, slowly rotating cloud of gas and dust began to come together. It was not unlike many interstellar clouds we see today, including the Orion nebula.

Our solar system probably formed from a vast cloud of gas and dust (upper left). *This cloud collapsed and began spinning around a central bulge* (far left). *The central bulge became the sun, and swirling eddies of gas and dust continued to orbit around it* (left). *These whirlpools of gas and dust eventually formed into the planets* (below).

No one is sure what caused the cloud to collapse on itself. One plausible theory says that the explosion of a nearby star sent shock waves across interstellar space and triggered the collapse.

As it collapsed, the rotating cloud began to spin faster and faster, the way figure-skaters spin faster when they draw their arms in. The cloud continued to contract and whirl until it formed a spinning disk the size of our solar system. Scientists call this disk of gas and dust the solar nebula. At the center of the nebula was a relatively dense bulge that would eventually form into the sun.

The collapse of the interstellar cloud created a great deal of heat, and soon after it formed, the solar nebula was quite hot. In its inner regions, interstellar dust grains were probably vaporized by the intense heat. The center of the nebula got hottest, and when temperatures reached some 18,000,000° F. (10,000,000° C), thermonuclear reactions were triggered in the central bulge, and the sun was born.

FIRE AND ICE

Meanwhile, the nebula itself was condensing and forming various substances. Because temperatures varied across the nebula, different substances formed at different distances from the sun. In the outermost regions, far from the infant sun, volatile compounds such as water, ammonia, and methane, which vaporize between 212° F. and 572° F. (100° C and 300° C), condensed to form ice crystals. Closer in, temperatures of about 1,800° F. (1,000° C) were too high for ice to form but low

enough for grains of silicate dust to condense. Still closer to the newborn sun, iron, aluminum, and titanium, which vaporize between 4,440° F. and 5,916° F. (2,467° C and 3,287° C), condensed into grains of metal.

We see the effects of this temperature range today. In the inner solar system, we find dense, rocky bodies. Earth, Venus, and Mercury are the richest in metal, similar in density, and presumably started out with similar compositions. But as we shall see, torrid Venus turned out very differently from Earth. Moving farther out, we find Mars, a rocky planet less dense than Earth. Beyond Mars are the asteroids—leftover chunks of rock and metal. And in the outer solar system, gas and ice dominate. Jupiter, Saturn, Uranus, and Neptune are rich in the lightest elements hydrogen and helium, while their satellites are rich in ice.

THE BIRTH OF THE PLANETS

As the nebula condensed, small bodies called planetesimals took form. Within a few thousand years, there were millions of these bodies circling the infant sun, each a few miles across. Planetesimals collided and stuck together, and within a few million years grew to be perhaps 60 miles (100 kilometers) across. Their gravity attracted more debris, and the embryonic planets slowly grew to their present size.

During this period, the planets were subjected to an unending rain of debris. According to researchers, this bombardment was so violent that the surfaces of the solid planets may have become completely melted. After their surfaces cooled and solidified again, the newly formed planets quickly swept up the last wandering planetesimals, producing the crater-covered surfaces seen on Mercury, the moon, Mars, and the satellites of Jupiter and Saturn.

The record of this violent bombardment has been erased on Earth by geologic activity. On the moon, Mercury, and Mars, only part of the early record was erased before these planets grew cold and their geologic activity ceased.

COMETS: GIVERS OF LIFE

At the fringes of the solar nebula, where the temperature was cold, condensation formed the fluffy lumps we call comets. This material was unaltered by the subsequent history of the system, and these frozen wanderers may hold the key to deciphering the earliest events in the solar system's formation. They may allow us to reach back 5 billion years or more in time in order to find out what things were like in the early solar nebula. They may also have been responsible for life itself. Even as Earth and the other solid planets were forming, comets had formed at the solar system's edge. The gravity of Jupiter and other massive planets probably attracted many comets into the inner solar system. Earth and the other solid planets swept up these comets, incorporating their water and other elements.

The moon, Mars, Venus, and Mercury appear to have lost most or all of this supply of water and other elements. But Earth held onto these elements in the form of an atmosphere and oceans, allowing life to arise.

OTHER SUNS, OTHER PLANETS

The interstellar cloud that spawned the solar nebula may have contained a thousand times the total mass of our solar system. It may have fragmented to produce a number of stars and solar systems. Stars are being born from such clouds even today, and there may be planets around some of them. Most importantly, the formation of planets seems to be a natural occurrence. Nothing special is required. Astronomers feel sure that out of the billions of stars in our own galaxy, there must be many with planets around them. And the laws of probability indicate that some of these may harbor life.

The search for other planets is one of astronomy's most exciting challenges. While no confirmed extrasolar planets have been found, astronomers have detected clouds of dust around stars that may be other solar systems in the making. And while optical telescopes search for other planets, astronomers are using giant radio telescopes to search for signals from other civilizations.

Still, there are plenty of wonderful and fascinating worlds within our own solar system that should hold astronomers' interests for years to come. It is to these planets, moons, asteroids, and comets that we now turn our attention.

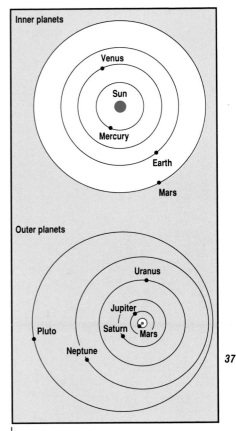

37

The orbits of the nine planets are shown in this double diagram. The top diagram plots the orbits of the four inner, terrestrial planets. The lower one depicts the orbits of the four gaseous planets and Pluto.

The planets are drawn to a scale at the right relative to their sizes, ranging from Jupiter, the largest, to Pluto, the smallest. If they were to be drawn to a scale relative to the distances between them, the sun being the size of a half dollar, then Pluto would be about 420 feet (126 meters) away.

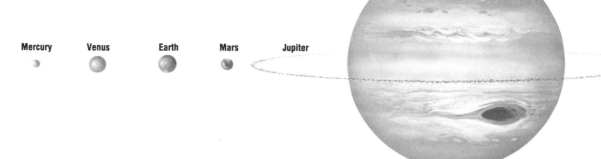

Mercury   Venus   Earth   Mars   Jupiter

Saturn   Uranus   Neptune   Pluto

If each of the planets were visible from Pluto (lower right), our solar system might look something like this. The sun is approximately 3.7 billion miles (5.9 billion kilometers) away.

EARTH AND THE MOON

Earth is enclosed in a bluish envelope of air, called the atmosphere, which extends as far as 1,000 miles (1,600 kilometers) above the surface.

EARTH

If you were approaching the sun from another star, you probably wouldn't notice the small planet called Earth. Huge Jupiter might catch your eye first. Or perhaps Saturn, with its beautiful system of rings, would attract your attention. But if, in your wanderings, you visited the third world out from the sun, you would

The workings of both nature and humans are evident in landforms on Earth. This satellite photograph of Medicine Hat in Alberta, Canada, shows the carving effects of rivers and streams, the quiltwork appearance of cultivated fields, and the crisscrossing of city and country streets and roads.

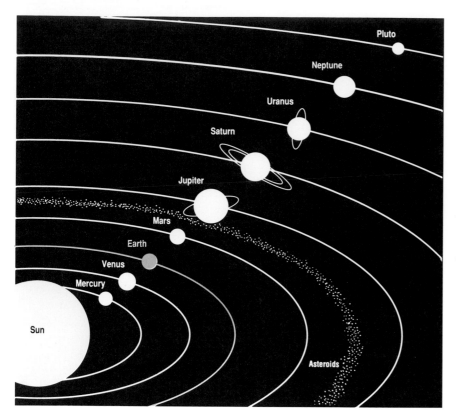

find that it is unlike any other in the solar system. The most important difference can be said in a single word: life. No other planet is known to harbor living things.

This is no coincidence. Conditions on Earth are just right for life as we know it. Our atmosphere contains the right mixture of gases. Temperatures are moderate over most of the planet. And that precious substance called water is plentiful in liquid form.

Earth itself is alive with geologic activity. Wind and water are in constant motion, changing the face of the land. The land itself is stirring, with ranges of mountains being pushed up and volcanoes pouring forth molten rock to make new land. From its beginning, Earth has been an active planet.

What was that beginning? The Earth's crust has changed so much over the eons that all traces of our planet's birth and infancy have been erased. The oldest rocks found on Earth are 4.3 billion years old, yet geologists know that our planet, and the rest of the solar system, formed some 800 million years earlier. For scientists, piecing together that missing history and the story of Earth's origin requires painstaking detective work.

How Earth Began

According to current ideas, Earth, like the sun and the other planets, condensed out of a cloud of gas and dust that slowly began to contract roughly 4.6 billion years ago. As the cloud shrank, some of the dust grains, coated with a fluffy layer of frozen cloud material, gently collided and stuck together. More and more grains collided and accumulated. Soon there were a number of small, solid lumps called planetesimals orbiting amid the gas and dust, and these collided with each other to form still bigger fragments.

Within a few thousand years, enough planetesimals collided to form an embryonic planet several miles across. A hundred million years or so later, our world had grown to roughly its present size. Its interior was a fairly uniform mixture of dust and frozen gases. But it did not stay that way.

Each particle that collided with the growing Earth added some energy to the planet. More heat came from the decay of radioactive elements (like isotopes of potassium, thorium, and uranium) in its interior. Eventually, temperatures climbed so high that Earth's interior melted completely through.

Imagine this molten planet that existed some 4.5 billion years ago. Within the liquid, elements of different density separated: heavier components, such as iron and nickel, sank to the middle of Earth, while lighter ones such as silicon, aluminum, and magnesium, stayed closer to the surface. Lightest of all were gases such as nitrogen, hydrogen, and oxygen.

These lightest components rose to the uppermost layers of the molten interior. Later on, these gases escaped to the surface through volcanoes and became part of the atmosphere. The water vapor condensed to form Earth's oceans. About 3.7 billion years ago, photosynthesis by early organisms began changing carbon dioxide in the atmosphere into oxygen. Most of the

rest became incorporated in limestones and other carbonate rocks.

The Structure of Earth

What lies within Earth today? Geologists have explored the planet's interior by studying volcanoes and volcanic rocks, by examining the composition of meteorites, and by investigating earthquakes. When an earthquake occurs, it sends seismic waves through Earth. These waves change in frequency and intensity as they pass through the different layers of the planet. From their analyses of earthquakes, geologists believe Earth is comprised of three main components—the core, the mantle, and the crust.

The core, with a radius of approximately 2,200 miles (3,500

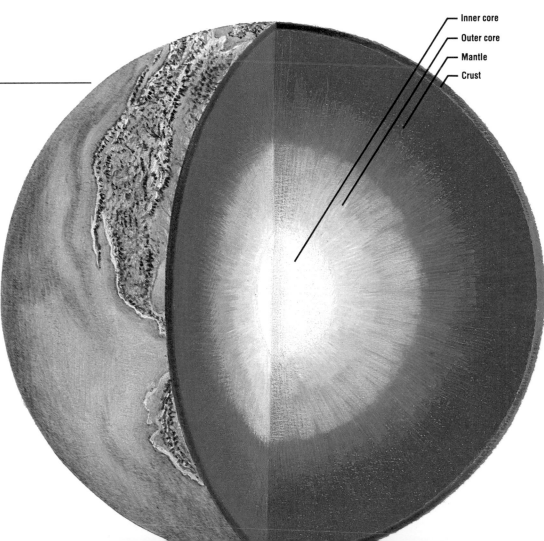

Inner core

Outer core

Mantle

Crust

43

This cross section of Earth's interior shows the inner composition of the planet. Beneath the crust is a mantle of solid rock, ranging in temperature from 1,600°F. (870°C) at the top to 4,000°F. (2,200°C) near the bottom. Farther down is the outer core, a layer of molten iron and nickel, its temperature climbing to 9,000°F. (5,000°C) in the deepest parts. At the center of Earth is an inner core of solid iron and nickel with a temperature that may be as high as 9,000°F. (5,000°C).

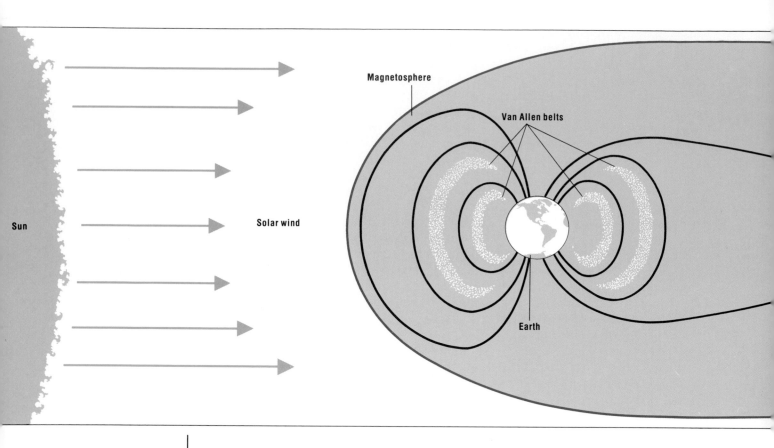

Magnetosphere

Van Allen belts

Solar wind

Sun

Earth

Earth's magnetism operates in a region called the magnetosphere. Radiation from the sun acts like a wind that blows the magnetosphere into a long tail. The magnetosphere includes the Van Allen belts, which consist of large numbers of charged electrons and protons trapped by the magnetism.

kilometers), is probably a mixture of iron and nickel. The center of Earth is still very hot—so hot that the outer portion of the core is actually metallic liquid. The motion of this fluid as Earth rotates may be the cause of the planet's magnetic field. The inner part of the core is also extremely hot, but the immense weight of the rest of Earth squeezes it into a solid ball.

The mantle, which is approximately 1,800 miles (2,900 kilometers) thick, forms most of the outer half of Earth. It is made of dense rocks rich in magnesium, iron, and silicon. The outermost portion of the mantle is somewhat soft, like pitch, and it actually circulates in huge, slow-moving currents beneath the crust. This convection in the upper mantle is the means by which the intense heat of Earth's interior is carried to the surface.

The crust is the rigid, outermost layer of Earth. It is broken up into a series of plates that ac-tually move across the face of the globe, propelled by the convection currents in the upper mantle. The continents and ocean floors, which ride atop these plates, are in constant motion, but you would never notice—they move about as fast as your fingernails grow. Millions of years ago, the continents occupied very different positions than they do today.

The Ever-Changing Crust

Two types of crust cover Earth: the oceanic crust and the continental crust. The oceanic crust, which forms the ocean floors, is mainly made of medium-dense igneous rocks—basalt, gabbro, and periotite. Oceanic crust is about 5 miles (8 kilometers) thick on the average.

At vast fissures in the ocean floor, called mid-ocean ridges, molten rock flows out from the mantle to form new crust. Over millions of years, the ocean floor

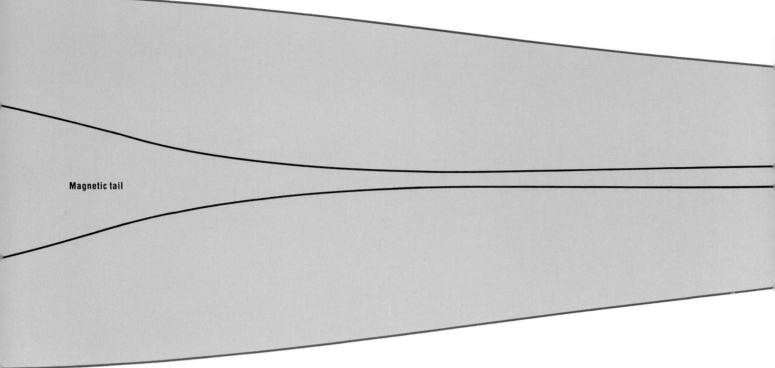

Magnetic tail

crawls away from this ridge like a conveyor belt, until it meets one of many great trenches called subduction zones. At the subduction zones, older crust actually descends into the mantle, where it melts and is recycled for new crust. Because oceanic crust is constantly being recycled, the oldest rocks on the ocean floor are only about 200 million years old—youthful compared to the 4.6-billion-year-old Earth.

In addition to the rocks that lie under the ocean, the continental crust has another layer of lighter, silicon-rich granite, plus further layers of a wide variety of fairly lightweight rocks. It is also quite a bit thicker than the oceanic crust, with an average of 25 miles (40 kilometers). Under some mountain ranges, the crust is as much as 55 miles (90 kilometers) thick.

Because the upper layer of the continental crust is of very low density, it is too buoyant to be dragged down with the descending crustal plate underneath. So, the continents ride atop the crustal plates, grinding past each other in some places (causing earthquakes in the process) and colliding to form great mountain belts (such as the Himalayas) in others. Some recycling may take place, but it is not nearly as dramatic as that of the oceanic crust.

Most of Earth's large-scale features, including mountain ranges, rifts in the crust, and chains of volcanic islands, can be explained by the motions of the crustal plates, a process that geologists call plate tectonics.

The planet we call home is special, not just because it is our home, but because it is an active, evolving world. As we shall see, Earth has outlived most of the other solid planets, whose internal fires apparently died out long ago, leaving cold, dead worlds. Earth is, by comparison, the jewel of the solar system.

45

Pythagoras · W. Bond · Strabo
Sea of Cold
(Mare Frigoris) · Endymion
Bay of Dew · Plato · Aristoteles · Hercules · Atlas
Juta Mountains · Alpine Valley
Bay of Rainbows · Straight Range · Mount Pico · Alps · Eudoxus · Franklin · Messala
Mairan · Sea of Rains (Mare Imbrium) · Aristillus · Caucasus · Lake of Dreams · Geminus
Archimedes · Autolycus · Posidonius · Taurus Mountains · Cleomedes
Struve · Aristarchus · Timocharis · Marsh of Decay · Apollo 15 landing · Macrobius
Ocean of Storms (Oceanus Procellarum) · Sea of Serenity (Mare Serenitatis) · Sea of Crises (Mare Crisium)
Carpathians · Apennines · Apollo 17 landing · Marsh of Sleep
Cardanus · Copernicus · Eratosthenes · Sea of Vapors (Mare Vaporum) · Haemus Mountains · Plinius · Marginal Sea
Riccioli · Kepler · Seething Bay · Manilius · Sea of Tranquility (Mare Tranquillitatis) · Foaming Sea
Reinhold · Julius Caesar · Agrippa · Maskelyne · Smyth's Sea
Lansberg · Central Bay · Schmidt · Apollo 11 landing · Sea of Fertility (Mare Fecunditatis)
Grimaldi · Apollo 12 landing · Hipparchus · Delambre · Gutenberg · Langrenus · Goclenius
Letronne · Riphaeus Mountains · Apollo 14 landing · Apollo 16 landing · Theophilus · Pyrenees · Colombo
Fra Mauro · Ptolemaeus · Albategnius · Cyrillus · Sea of Nectar (Mare Nectaris) · Vendelinus
Gassendi · Alphonsus · Abulfeda · Santbech · Petavius
Mersenius · Arzachel · Catharina · Altai Scarp · Fracastorius · Humboldt
Sea of Moisture (Mare Humorum) · Sea of Clouds (Mare Nubium) · Straight Wall · Piccolomini · Furnerius
Mercator · Pitatus · Purbach · Maurolycus · Janssen
Campanus · Regiomontanus · Walter · Pitiscus
Deslandres · Orontius · Stöffler · Vlacq
Schickard · Wilhelm · Tycho · Maginus · Curtius · Manzinus
Longomontanus · Clavius · Cuvier
Schiller · Scheiner · Blancanus

46

THE MOON

Our nearest neighbor in space has awed humanity from the beginning of time. Through the ages, the moon has been a god to some, a demon to others, and a mystery to all. Whether a half-circle bathed in the blue of an afternoon sky, a slender crescent hovering above the treetops at dusk, or a round, midnight beacon shining at full strength overhead, the moon dominates our skies. Today we view the moon not as a spirit, but as another world. What do we know of this alien body?

To the naked eye, the moon is a collection of light and dark patches. To many, the pattern resembles a face—the face of the man in the moon. To some, the moon has appeared to be a smooth, polished crystal sphere.

When Galileo turned his new telescope on the moon in 1609, he saw surprising new details. The surface was not smooth, as it looks from Earth, but covered with holes, which we call craters. Galileo saw that the dark

The nearside of the moon is the only side we ever see from Earth. This is because the moon turns once on its axis in the same time that it circles Earth, thus always keeping the same side facing Earth.

The following are labels on the moon map:

Schwarzschild, Sommerfeld, Rowland, Birkhoff, Compton, D'Alembert, Fowler, Landau, H. G. Wells, Campbell, Charlier, Wiener, Fabry, Shajn, Larmor, Cockcroft, Kovalevskaya, Joule, Moscow Sea (Mare Moscoviense), Trumpler, Fitzgerald, Freundlich, Dante, Vernadsky, Morse, Mach, Poynting, Anderson, Fersman, Fleming, Kekulé, Ostwald, Tsander, Guyot, Mendeleev, Hertzsprung, Schuster, Chaplygin, Daedalus, Icarus, Korolev, Keeler, Heaviside, Doppler, Paschen, Pasteur, Aitken, Galois, Hilbert, Tsiolkovsky, Fermi, Gagarin, Eastern Sea (Mare Orientale), Levi-Civita, Pavlov, Van de Graaff, Milne, Chebyshev, Southern Sea (Mare Australe), Jules Verne, Sea of Ingenuity (Mare Ingenii), Oppenheimer, Apollo, Mendel, Roche, Leibnitz, Von Kármán, Planck, Poincaré, Boltzmann, Antoniadi, Schrödinger, Zeeman, Cordilleras Rook Mountains

47

patches were smoother than the brighter, heavily cratered areas. Believing these smooth areas to be seas, he named them *maria* (singular, *mare*), the Latin word for seas.

In the centuries following Galileo, the moon was a new world to explore for astronomers armed with ever larger telescopes. By the middle of this century, they had seen that our satellite is a very different place than Earth. The moon has no atmosphere, no life. The maria turned out to be seas, not of water, but of hardened lava. And thousands of craters cover the barren, unchanging moonscape.

For many years, scientists lost interest in the moon. But by the middle of this century, astronomers realized that the moon is a museum piece of priceless value. All the processes that have erased the earliest geologic record of Earth—erosion by wind and water, distortion of the crust by folding, recycling of the crust by plate tectonics—are absent on the moon. On its crater-pocked surface is written the early history of our solar system, and the tale is a violent one.

The Moon's Violent Past

After the sun and planets formed, the solar system was filled with leftover debris. Each planet was a wandering target for chunks of rock called meteoroids. Meteoroids slammed into the moon at such high speeds that they blasted great holes, called impact craters, in the crust. Craters are the most common landform on the moon and, for that matter, in the entire solar system.

For nearly a billion years, meteoroids of all sizes rained onto the lunar surface, creating thousands of craters. Then, about 4 billion years ago, the bombardment died down. Today, small meteorite particles still strike the moon's surface. However, impacts by large bodies are a rare occurrence. But a look through a small telescope or a pair of binoculars shows the scars of the earlier, more violent era.

One of the more prominent lunar impact craters is Copernicus, which was formed roughly 900 million years ago. An explosion with as much energy as 20 trillion tons of TNT created this crater, 56 miles (90 kilometers) wide, in a matter of seconds. And Copernicus is only a medium-sized crater.

The largest craters, called impact basins, are hundreds of miles (kilometers) across. The impacts that formed these must have been truly colossal. After the basins formed, lava rose through cracks in the moon's crust and flooded their centers, creating the maria. Subsequent smaller impacts formed craters on these smooth lava plains.

The distribution of lava plains on the moon is puzzling to scientists. Almost all are on the side that always faces Earth (called the nearside). Only a few

This composite photograph of the moon shows the wide variety in size and shape of lunar craters.

48

are on the far side. This uneven distribution has not been completely explained. It may be that the nearside crust is thinner than that of the far side. If so, lavas from the interior may have broken through to the surface more easily on the nearside than the far side.

The Message in Moon Rocks

In 1969, astronauts landed on the moon and brought back treasures of incredible value—lunar rocks. Now scientists could study the moon directly instead of just in photographs. The lunar samples showed that the moon's surface is very, very old. The youngest lunar rocks yet analyzed—volcanic rocks called basalts from the maria—are 3.2 billion years old.

The heavily cratered highlands contain some of the oldest rocks on the moon—formed about 4.4 billion years ago, just 200 million years later than the solar system itself. By comparison, the oldest rocks yet found on Earth are only 3.8 billion years old. Geologists believe the moon became so hot during its formation that its upper layers became molten. Lighter minerals floated to the surface and formed a crust made of a rock called anorthosite. The highlands are the remains of that early lunar crust.

Over billions of years, impacts have changed the original crust. Samples of the old anorthosites are hard to find. Another type of rock is more common—breccia,

Hipparchus (180 B.C.?–125 B.C.?) was an ancient Greek astronomer who calculated the length of the year to within six minutes. His observations of Earth, the moon, and the sun greatly influenced later astronomers, including Ptolemy.

which is a collection of dust and rock fragments welded together by the heat and pressure of a meteoroid impact. Many of the rocks in and around impact craters are breccias.

Where Did the Moon Come From?

The most basic question about the moon—how it formed—is still unanswered. Some scientists believe the moon broke away from Earth while our planet was still molten. But it is difficult to explain how the material that formed the moon was able to escape from Earth in the first place.

Other scientists have proposed that the moon and Earth formed separately from the same cloud

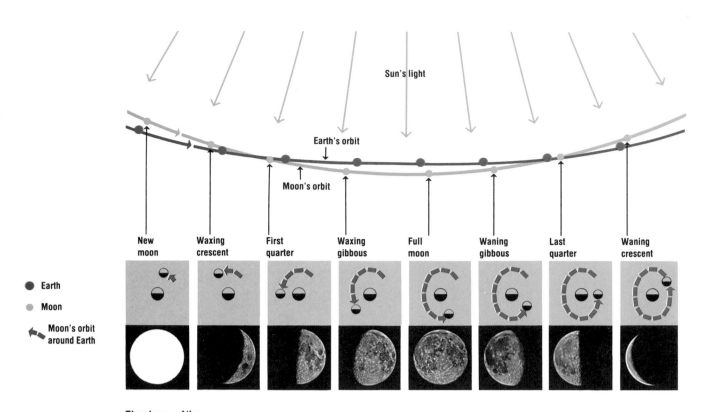

Sun's light

Earth's orbit

Moon's orbit

| New moon | Waxing crescent | First quarter | Waxing gibbous | Full moon | Waning gibbous | Last quarter | Waning crescent |

● Earth

● Moon

◀ Moon's orbit around Earth

The phases of the moon are caused by the moon's orbit around Earth as Earth and the moon travel around the sun. Half of the moon is always in sunlight, but varying amounts of the lighted side are visible from Earth. As the moon and Earth move along their orbits, more of the sunlit part is seen, until it shines as a full moon. Then less and less of the sunlit part is seen until the dark new moon returns.

of gas and dust. The problem here is that the moon's composition is somewhat different from that of Earth, a fact that is difficult to explain if both bodies came from the same source material.

A third theory holds that the moon originally formed far from Earth but later wandered close enough to be captured by our planet's gravity. The problem here lies in explaining how such a capture occurred and where in the solar system it formed to have its present composition.

Recently, a theory proposed in the mid-1970's has gained the greatest acceptance from astronomers. In this view, the interior of the young Earth melted, forming an iron-rich core and an iron-poor outer half (the mantle). Sometime later, one of the large meteoroids, perhaps thousands of miles across, struck Earth and blasted a cloud of debris from our planet's upper layers into space. This cloud ultimately condensed to form an iron-poor moon with some of the chemical properties of Earth's mantle.

Compared to Earth, the moon is a primitive, unevolved body. It was once believed that the moon was of the same composition throughout. Since the lunar landings, we now know that the moon, like the planets, is composed of layers. There is a thin crust, perhaps 35 to 60 miles (56 to 96 kilometers) thick. There is a mantle, homogeneous in composition, that extends to approximately 185 to 310 miles (296 to 496 kilometers) toward the center. The core, which is small, may be iron-rich, but nonmolten.

Unlike Earth, the moon lacked the necessary bulk to retain its heat for long. After the last of the mare basalts oozed onto the surface about 3 billion years ago, the moon was essentially a dead world, almost exactly as we see it today. Fortunately, it has much to tell us of its past, as well as our own.

50

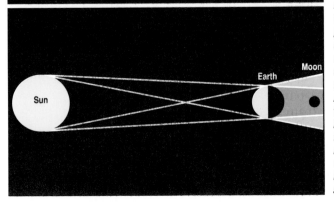

A solar eclipse (top) occurs when the moon passes between the sun and Earth. The sun cannot be seen from areas on Earth that lie in the moon's shadow. A lunar eclipse (bottom) takes place when Earth is directly between the sun and the moon. The moon is invisible while moving through Earth's shadow.

From Earth, you can see either a solar or a lunar eclipse (diagram to the left). But from the moon (above) an eclipse of Earth is not possible. This is because the moon is too small and too far away for its shadow to eclipse Earth. At most, you might be able to see the tip of the moon's shadow cone moving across the surface of Earth.

Mercury

MERCURY

Imagine discovering a new planet overnight. That is essentially what happened to scientists in 1974, when the United States spacecraft *Mariner 10* flew past Mercury. Until then, this planet closest to the sun—roughly two-fifths the size of Earth—had been seen as no more than a tiny, almost featureless blur in even the largest telescopes. From Earth, Mercury can often be seen at dawn or dusk. However, it is sometimes difficult to find because it never strays far from the glare of the sun.

Mercury is a world ruled by the sun. If you could stand on its surface, the sun would be a fiery disk two and one-half times bigger than seen from Earth. The sky would be black, for Mercury

has only the barest wisp of an atmosphere. No blanket of air shields Mercury's surface from the sun's intense heat and deadly radiation. During the day, temperatures soar as high as 648° F. (342° C). Human explorers would find it extremely difficult to survive, even in space suits. At night, temperatures plummet to −315° F. (−193° C). Mercury is clearly a world of extremes.

All this was known before *Mariner 10* flew past Mercury. Astronomers also knew that the planet's density is unusually high—more than five times that of water—which implies that Mercury has a large, iron-rich core. And by bouncing radar waves off the planet, they had determined that Mercury rotates

In this photograph, taken by a telescope on Earth, tiny Mercury is seen against the awesome background of the sun. The sun is more than 280 times as large as Mercury.

once every 59 earth-days. But what was Mercury's surface like? Did it have craters such as those on the moon? How much had Mercury evolved since its formation? Until *Mariner 10's* arrival, little could be said to answer these questions.

Mariner 10 ended Mercury's reign as an unknown world. In its three fly-bys, the robot explorer sent back detailed pictures of almost half the planet. It confirmed the high surface temperatures and found a weak magnetic field.

The pictures show a barren world that, like the moon, is covered with impact craters. The fact that there are so many craters means that much of Mercury's surface is very old, probably close to the age of the solar system itself.

Unlike the moon, the portion of Mercury photographed by *Mariner 10* has few large impact basins, and almost no broad lava seas. One large, spectacular basin, called Caloris, was found. It is a multiringed crater some 800 miles (1,280 kilometers) in diameter. Within Caloris are lava plains that resemble the lunar maria. These lavas must have flooded the basin sometime after it was blasted out of Mercury's crust.

Many of Mercury's craters have smooth areas between them that also look like volcanic plains. Some may indeed be lava, or they may be blankets of debris ejected from nearby impact craters. The origin of these smooth intercrater plains is still unknown.

Mariner 10 found surprising, fascinating features—a number of clifflike ridges stretching thousands of miles across Mercury. Some of these scarps cut right through impact craters. Geologists believe the scarps were created early in Mercury's history, after the planet's crust had formed but before the interior had cooled off. As the interior cooled, it shrank, causing the solid crust to shrink also. The scarps are the scars of that shrinkage, which probably reduced Mercury's diameter by 1 to 2.5 miles (1.6 to 4.0 kilometers).

Mercury appears to be a primitive world. Like Earth, Mercury probably became hot enough to melt soon after it formed, and its material separated into layers. But geologists do not think Mercury evolved much further before its interior cooled down. The planet appears to have died geologically early in its history.

Mercury was photographed in detail for the first time by Mariner 10 in 1974. Eighteen photographs were computer-enhanced and put together to make this photomosaic of the planet's cratered surface.

Mercury at a glance

Mercury, shown in orange in the diagram, is the closest planet to the sun.

Distance from sun: *Shortest*—28.6 million miles (46 million kilometers); *Greatest*—43 million miles (69.2 million kilometers); *Mean*—36 million miles (57.9 million kilometers).

Distance from earth: *Shortest*—57 million miles (57.9 million kilometers); *Greatest*—136 million miles (218.9 million kilometers).

Diameter: 3,031 miles (4,878 kilometers).

Length of year: 88 earth-days.

Rotation period: 59 earth-days.

Temperature: —315° to 648° F. (— 193° to 342° C).

Atmosphere: Helium, hydrogen, oxygen.

Number of satellites: None.

Venus, as seen from Earth, is brighter than any other planet or star. At certain times of the year, Venus is the first planet or star that can be seen in the western sky in the evening. At other times, it is the last planet or star that can be seen in the eastern sky in the morning.

VENUS

Venus has long been a world shrouded in mystery. Brilliant yellowish-white clouds completely surround the planet, hiding its surface from our view. For decades, astronomers knew nothing about Venus except its most basic attributes. In size and density, Venus is almost a twin of Earth. Was it possible that beneath the clouds, another Earth existed? Astronomers knew that Venus, being roughly 30 percent closer to the sun than Earth, would be a good deal warmer. Perhaps, some speculated, Venus was covered with tropical forests, much like the prehistoric Earth. They couldn't have been more wrong.

When the American space probe *Mariner 2* flew by Venus in 1962, it sent back verification of data collected earlier by radio astronomers: Venus' carbon dioxide atmosphere was far too hot to support life. More details on the mysterious world were slow in coming. Finally, in the 1970's, the Soviet Union's *Venera* probes landed on Venus and sent back the first reports from its surface. They found truly hellish conditions: a bare, rock-strewn landscape lay beneath crushing atmospheric pressure 90 times that on Earth's surface—equivalent to pressures found in the depths of Earth's oceans—at a scorching temperature of 850° F. (455° C). In fact, Venus is far hotter than its sunward neighbor, Mercury.

THE GREENHOUSE PLANET

Why is Venus so hot? The answer is that the planet's massive carbon dioxide atmosphere acts like a greenhouse. The glass walls of a greenhouse allow sunlight to pass through, warming its contents during the day. Objects inside reemit the energy as heat, but the glass does not transmit this infrared (heat) radiation. As a result, greenhouses stay warm even when their surroundings are cool. Because carbon dioxide readily absorbs infrared radiation, Venus' greenhouse is a very efficient one, maintaining the planet's extremely high temperatures. The dense blanket of gases and high-speed winds also carry heat to the planet's night side, which is almost as hot as the day side.

Venus could not be any less Earthlike. Yet, scientists find it puzzling that two planets as similar in size and mass should have turned out so differently. One important fact seems to be Venus' lack of liquid water, which strongly influences climate. Venus may have started

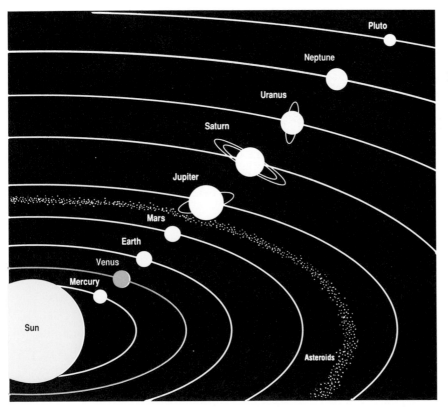

Venus at a glance

Venus, shown in orange in the diagram, is the second closest planet to the sun.

Distance from sun: *Shortest*—66,800,000 mi. (107,500,000 km); *Greatest*—67,700,000 mi. (109,000,000 km); *Mean*—67,250,000 mi. (108,230,000 km).

Distance from earth: *Shortest*—25,000,000 mi. (40,200,000 km); *Greatest*—160,000,000 mi. (257,000,000 km).

Diameter: 7,520 mi. (12,100 km).

Length of year: 225 earth-days.

Rotation period: 243 earth-days.

Temperature: 850° F. (455° C).

Atmosphere: Carbon dioxide, nitrogen, water vapor, argon, carbon monoxide, neon, sulfur dioxide.

Number of satellites: None.

out with nearly as much water in its bulk as Earth did. But it may be that, due to the planet's nearness to the sun, virtually all of Venus' water was rapidly boiled off into the atmosphere, where it was then broken down by sunlight and irretrievably lost. We can be very thankful for the fact that Earth held onto its supply of water; if it hadn't, a carbon-dioxide atmosphere and Venuslike conditions would surely have developed. But as it turned out, most of Earth's carbon dioxide is contained in limestone rocks or is dissolved in the oceans.

Today, the atmosphere on Venus is nearly all carbon dioxide, with small amounts of nitrogen and only minute amounts of sulfur dioxide, water vapor, carbon monoxide, and other gases. There are even traces of hydrochloric acid.

Were you able to stand on Venus' surface, you would not see the sun. Instead, the sky would be an unbroken, brightly lit cloudscape. Because the thick atmosphere absorbs all but the redder wavelengths of sunlight, everything would look orange, as if you were wearing tinted sunglasses. Even in a well-insulated, pressure-resistant spacecraft, you probably would not want to stay long. Venus is not a very inviting world.

Venus' atmosphere receives so much energy from the sun and the greenhouse effect that it races around the planet once every four Earth-days. For comparison, the planet itself takes 243 Earth-days to spin once on its axis. In addition, Venus is the only known world that rotates from east to west, the opposite direction of Earth and the other planets. This odd retrograde (backward) rotation has not yet been conclusively explained.

In visible light, the clouds are featureless. But seen in the ultraviolet, they display broad, Y-shaped patterns caused by the atmosphere's swift motion.

This panorama of the surface of Venus was taken by the Soviet space probe **Venera 14** in 1982. Portions of the descent module appear in the foreground.

Though study of the Venusian atmosphere is still in its beginnings, scientists hope to find clues to the behavior of our own atmosphere by studying that of Venus.

BENEATH THE CLOUDS

What lies beneath the gleaming white clouds? There is an answer, for scientists have finally lifted the Venusian veil—with radar. American and Soviet spacecraft orbiting Venus have used radar waves to penetrate the clouds and create a picture of the planet's surface. Ground-based radar systems have also contributed to this mapping process.

Interestingly, Venus has relatively few impact craters. On a large scale, it looks surprisingly like Earth: low plains similar to Earth's ocean floors cover much of the globe. These are broken here and there by vast plateaus that resemble continents.

In more detailed views, Venus displays a host of complex and varied landforms, many unlike anything seen on Earth or other worlds. The continents contain jumbled, fractured mountain ranges, in some areas resembling the crinkled hide of an elephant. Some of Venus' mountains tower high into the broiling atmosphere, higher than Earth's Mount Everest. Enormous rifts in the Venusian crust have also been detected.

The radar pictures also show that Venus has been volcanically active. Lava flows are widespread, and huge features resembling shield volcanoes have been spotted. There are also broad, oval-shaped features that appear to be upwellings of lava at shallow depths in the Venusian crust.

Hardly anything is known of Venus' internal structure. Based on its calculated density and size, scientists believe the planet probably has a solid core composed largely of nickel and iron. Any liquid core must be quite small, since Venus possesses no magnetic field. Most of the planet's bulk is likely contained in a thick mantle, topped by a crust thought to be thicker than Earth's.

In 1982, two more *Venera* probes provided the first detailed chemical analyses of the surface. Each of the craft drilled into the surface, extracted a small sample, and analyzed it in a sophisticated on-board laboratory. The results show that the places where the *Veneras* landed are covered with rocks similar in composition to volcanic rocks called basalts that are found on Earth.

A PRIMITIVE EARTH?

As yet, scientists have no solid evidence that Venus' crust may be broken up into moving plates like Earth's. Like the moon and Mercury, it may be another one-plate planet, but it has certainly been geologically active. It appears that the Venusian surface has been flooded by volcanic lavas, fractured, and folded. Fewer impact craters than expected have been found, suggesting either that meteors burn up before they can strike the surface, or that much of the planet's terrain formed less than a billion years ago. Venus' earlier history has almost surely been erased. And

58

These three photographs of Venus were taken at seven-hour intervals by Mariner 10 in 1974, showing how rapidly its thick cloud cover moves across the planet's surface. The feature indicated by the arrow is about 600 miles (1,000 kilometers) across.

it is quite possible that Venus is still active today. Some scientists believe that geologically Venus is just getting started. In that case, it may be much like the early Earth was.

Venus has not yielded easily to the curiosity of human beings. Its opaque clouds force us to use unusual methods for glimpses of its surface. Its hot, corrosive, crushing atmosphere destroys our space probes even as they radio their findings to Earth. Undaunted, scientists continue to dispatch new spacecraft to Venus. In 1985, two more Soviet *Venera* probes landed on the planet's nightside to report on conditions and analyze the surface. They were accompanied by French-made balloons that were released into the Venusian winds, sending back data on the upper atmosphere. And the United States is planning a radar-equipped orbiter to map the planet at high resolution sometime in the near future.

Venus goes through phases similar to those of the moon. However, in addition to changes in brightness and shape, Venus seems to change in size also. This is due to its changing distance from Earth. Venus appears largest when on the same side of the sun as Earth, at which time only a thin, sunlit crescent-area can be seen. Venus is smallest when on the opposite side of the sun from Earth, at which time almost all its sunlit area can be seen.

This photograph of Mars was taken by Viking 2 in 1976. Two wisps of clouds, thought to consist mostly of water vapor, can be seen. Situated near the top and at the bottom of the photograph, the clouds are next to dark spots, which are probably giant volcanoes. Between these two features and slightly to the right is a giant canyon scratched into the planet's surface.

MARS

No planet has captured human imagination more than Mars. The ancient Romans, awed by its reddish glow in the night sky, named the planet for their god of war. In more recent times, the red planet has been the favorite target of speculators and science-fiction writers who imagined vast civilizations there—the cities of Martians.

Mars occasionally comes to 48.7 million miles (78.4 million kilometers) from the Earth, closer to us than any planet except Venus. During these close approaches, anyone with a modest-sized telescope can see faint

Giovanni Schiaparelli (1835–1910) was an Italian astronomer who first detected dark lines on the surface of Mars.

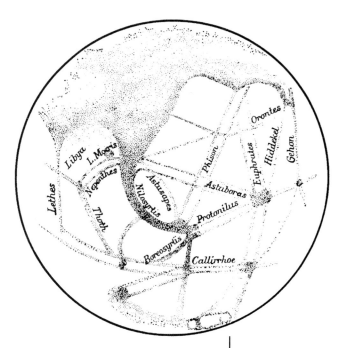

This composite map, based on sketches made by Schiaparelli in June, 1888, shows the canali (channels) he observed on the surface of Mars.

patches of dark gray on the pinkish surface. Often, an observer can glimpse patches of white at the planet's poles; these are icecaps that resemble Earth's. But our view of Mars has always been a frustrating one, for it never shows us more than slight detail.

CANALS ON MARS?

In 1877, when Mars made an especially good showing, Italian astronomer Giovanni Schiaparelli turned his telescope on the planet and reported seeing dark lines, which he called *canali,* on the surface. Schiaparelli said nothing of their origin; canali simply means *channels* in Italian. But somehow the word was translated into English as *canals.* If there were canals on Mars, then someone must have built them—or so thought Boston-born astronomer Percival Lowell.

Lowell was convinced that the canals were the work of a Martian civilization, used to transport water from the polar icecaps to their cities in the Martian deserts. Working at his observatory in Flagstaff, Arizona, he counted over 500 canals. Lowell died in 1916 without ever knowing if his Martians were real.

When bigger telescopes like the 200-inch (500-centimeter) reflector at Palomar Observatory in California were built, astronomers could see more detail on Mars than Lowell had seen. They found no evidence of canals or any other signs of civilization. But that didn't put an end to dreams of Martian life. A number of scientists interpreted the dark patches on Mars as vegetation, claiming to see changes in plant cover with the Martian seasons. Not until 1965 did the dreams of Mars as an Earthlike world finally die. That year a robot explorer called *Mariner 4* sped past Mars and radioed to Earth the first close-up pictures of its surface.

THE MARINERS TO MARS

Had Lowell been around to see *Mariner 4*'s pictures, he would have been surprised and perhaps heartbroken. Instead of civilizations and canals, only a barren, crater-pocked surface was seen. Mars looked no more inspiring than the moon. But *Mariner 4* had only glimpsed a tiny portion of the planet. Perhaps there might be more interesting sights on other parts of Mars. In 1971, scientists sent another automated explorer, *Mariner 9*, into orbit around the red planet for a better look.

Unfortunately, *Mariner 9* arrived during the height of a planet-wide dust storm. Such storms are common on Mars, but this one was especially severe. For weeks, the entire planet was hidden by a shroud of wind-blown dust. Finally, in late 1971, the dust began to clear.

The first features to appear amid the haze were four dark spots. Later pictures showed that the spots were in fact craters.

More dust settled, and it became clear that these craters were perched atop enormous mountains. Geologists realized the mountains were four huge volcanoes. The largest, named *Olympus Mons* (after the dwelling place of the gods of Greek legends), towers 15 miles (25 kilometers) above the surface, nearly three times as high as Mount Everest. Lava once poured from its summit crater, which is some 50 miles (80 kilometers) across. But today, there are no signs of activity from any of the Martian volcanoes. They may be dormant, or they may have died out millions or even billions of years ago.

More surprises followed. East of the four volcanoes, a vast canyon almost as long as the continental United States cut through the Martian crust. Geologists named the canyon *Valles Marineris*, after the spacecraft that showed us Mars's true nature.

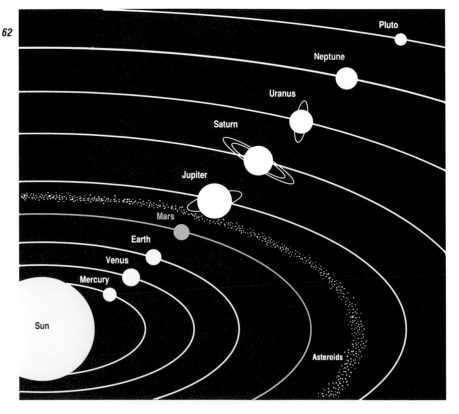

Mars at a glance

Mars, shown in orange in the diagram, is the next planet beyond the earth.

Distance from sun:
  Shortest—128,500,000 miles (206,800,000 kilometers);
  Greatest—154,900,000 miles (249,200,000 kilometers);
  Mean—141,700,000 miles (228,000,000 kilometers).

Distance from earth:
  Shortest—48,700,000 miles (78,390,000 kilometers);
  Greatest—248,000,000 miles (399,000,000 kilometers).

Diameter: 4,200 miles (6,790 kilometers).

Length of year: About 1 earth-year and 10.5 months.

Rotation period: 24 hours and 37 minutes.

Temperature: −191° to −24° F. (−124° to −31° C).

Atmosphere: Carbon dioxide, nitrogen, argon, oxygen, carbon monoxide, neon, krypton, xenon, and water vapor.

Number of satellites: 2.

Like the moon, Mars has thousands of impact craters of all sizes and a number of large impact basins filled with lava plains. And the crust of Mars—like the moon's, Mercury's, and Venus'—does not appear to be broken up into plates like Earth's. Strangely, Mars seems to be split into two halves—a northern region of volcanic plains and a southern region of crater-pocked uplands. Scientists have yet to explain this interesting phenomenon.

What of the light and dark markings seen from Earth? To no one's surprise, *Mariner 9* found that Mars is covered not with vegetation but with deposits of fine dust. These show up as bright areas in our telescopes. In some places, this dust has been swept away by the swift Martian winds to reveal the darker rocks beneath, accounting for most of the dark markings.

The handiwork of Martian winds—ranging from vast dune fields and streaklike deposits in the shelter of craters to occasional dust storms and dust devils—is seen over much of the planet. Over billions of years,

Mars has two satellites, Phobos and Deimos. Phobos (left) was photographed by the Mariner 9 probe. Viewed through a telescope (right), Phobos appears as a bright spot to the left of Mars. Deimos is fainter and farther away, to the right.

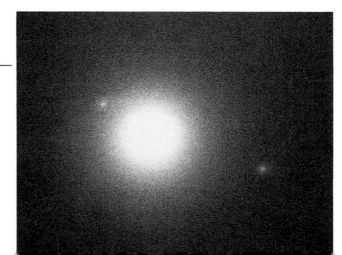

the erosive action of wind-blown dust has softened crater rims, mountains, and other landforms. But despite such erosive action, much of the ancient terrain has survived.

THE ANCIENT RIVERS OF MARS

One of *Mariner 9*'s most interesting discoveries was a set of channels (unrelated to Schiaparelli's channels) that look exactly like dry riverbeds seen on Earth. Scientists concluded the ones on Mars must surely have been carved by running water. Yet, no signs of liquid water are to be found on Mars today. In fact, the Martian atmosphere is so thin—with a surface pressure averaging about 100 times less than that at sea level on Earth—that a drop of water placed on Mars' surface would evaporate in seconds.

Furthermore, temperatures on Mars are usually far below the freezing point of water. At noon on a summer day at the Martian equator, the uppermost layer of dust might warm to $-24°$ F. $(-31°$ C). But most of the time, Mars is far colder. At the poles, temperatures drop to as low as $-191°$ F. $(-124°$ C), which is cold enough to freeze carbon dioxide, forming deposits of dry ice on the surface. The vast icecaps covering the poles are mixtures of frozen carbon dioxide and water ice.

Clearly, Mars was a very different place when the channels were formed. There must have been a far denser atmosphere, perhaps one made largely of carbon dioxide, which now comprises most of the thin Martian air. Perhaps over time, most of the carbon dioxide was incorporated into the crust, much like Earth's carbonate rocks.

Where is all of Mars' water now? Some of it is contained in the polar icecaps, but they don't account for enough to have carved the big channels. Many geologists think the rest could be frozen in the upper layers of Mars' crust. But no one will be certain until future spacecraft are sent to Mars with sensors to detect the buried ice, or until human explorers drill into the crust of Mars.

THE VIKINGS ON MARS

On July 20, 1976, a three-legged spacecraft called *Viking 1* descended through the thin atmosphere of Mars. As it neared the surface, the craft cast off its large, white parachute and fired three small retrorockets to slow its final few yards of descent. With a sudden bump, *Viking 1* came to a stop in the dust of Mars' *Chryse Planitia*—the Plain of Gold.

For scientists back on Earth, *Viking 1*'s landing brought something more valuable than gold— the first pictures and analyses made from the surface of Mars.

The Valles Marineris, *or Mariner Valleys, is a huge complex of canyons stretching for hundreds of miles across the surface of Mars. More than 100 TV images taken by Viking 1 were used to form this composite photomosaic.*

65

The images showed thousands of rocks strewn from horizon to horizon on a gently rolling plain. Dunelike deposits of fine dust lay only a few hundred feet from the lander. On September 3, 1976, *Viking 2* set down at Mars' *Utopia Planitia* (Utopian Plains) amid hundreds of rocks. On the distant horizon, the rim of an impact crater broke the monotony of an otherwise featureless plain.

The *Vikings* operated for more than two years on Mars, sending back a harvest of data on their surroundings, including weather reports and chemical analyses of the dust. Color-enhanced pictures showed that the yellowish-brown soil appears reddish-brown in the Martian atmosphere. The chemical analyses revealed that the color is caused by oxidized iron—otherwise known as rust. Because fine dust is suspended in the atmosphere, the Martian sky looks pink.

Along with cameras, weather instruments, and soil analyzers, the *Vikings* carried a very special instrument—a biology laboratory only 1 cubic foot (0.03 cubic meter) in size. With it, Viking scientists hoped to answer the nagging question of whether there is life on Mars. With no water available and no protection from the sun's deadly ultraviolet rays, Martian life would have to be unusually hardy. But the possibility could not be ruled out.

Each *Viking* used its mechanical arm to scoop up some of the soil and dump it into the biology instrument, where three separate tests were performed. One involved adding water to the dust and waiting to see what happened. Even a weak nutrient broth was injected into one sample, in hopes that any microbes living in the soil would multiply and their metabolic wastes be detected. Each of the tests gave peculiar results that almost mimicked the characteristic activity of microbes on Earth. But when all the data were in, scientists concluded that highly reactive minerals, not Martian microbes, were responsible. If there is life on Mars, it eluded the Viking probes, but the question is still open in the minds of some hopeful scientists.

THE NEW MARTIANS

The Mars of fact turned out to be very different from the Mars of imagination. It is a less romantic world, perhaps, but no less interesting. Mars will continue to draw our attention. Someday in the not too distant future, astronauts will probably visit Mars to help solve more of the red planet's mysteries. They will search for water, and they will search for life. Eventually, they will set up a permanent outpost on Mars, a way station for voyages farther out into the solar system. Then, there *will* be Martians, after all.

The Size and Color of Asteroids

Vesta

Hektor

Thetis

Nysa

Ceres

Eunomia

Davida

Laetitia

Psyche

Interamnia

Phobos

ASTEROIDS

In the late 1700's, astronomers began searching for a "missing planet." According to Bode's law, a formula that accurately predicted the distances of the known planets from the sun, there was a gap between Mars and Jupiter where a planet ought to be. However, no planet was known to be there. But on the first night of 1801, an Italian astronomer named Giuseppe Piazzi discovered a small world, only about 600 miles (960 kilometers) across, which was subsequently named Ceres. It was exactly where Bode's law said it should be: 257 million miles (414 million kilometers) from the sun. Apparently, the missing planet had been found. But in following years, more small bodies were found in the same part of the solar system. Astronomers called these bodies asteroids.

Shown to scale against a portion of the moon, asteroids vary in size and shape, from tiny, potato-shaped Nysa to huge, spherical Ceres. Phobos, lower left, a captured moon of Mars, may also be an asteroid.

Where did the asteroids come from? Could it be that they were fragments of a much larger world, torn apart by an explosion or some other disaster? For many years, this was the accepted explanation for the asteroids' origin. But today, astronomers believe that asteroids are leftover debris from the formation of the solar system.

Today, the orbits of more than 3,000 asteroids are known. They range in size from Ceres, the largest asteroid, to tiny objects perhaps no bigger than grains of dust. Most asteroids orbit the sun between Mars and Jupiter in a doughnut-shaped zone called the Asteroid Belt. Dozens more have been discovered in the inner solar system on paths that cross Earth's orbit. These are called Apollo asteroids. And two swarms of asteroids share an orbit with the giant planet Jupiter. This last group is the Trojan asteroids.

WHAT ARE ASTEROIDS LIKE?

Asteroids probably resemble Phobos and Deimos, the two moons of Mars. Scientists believe Phobos and Deimos may be asteroids that were captured by Mars's gravity. Phobos and Deimos are irregular, battered chunks of rock. Their surfaces

The Willamette meteorite was found in Oregon in 1902. It is the largest meteorite ever found in the United States, measuring almost 10 feet (30 centimeters) in length and weighing about 15.5 short tons (14 metric tons).

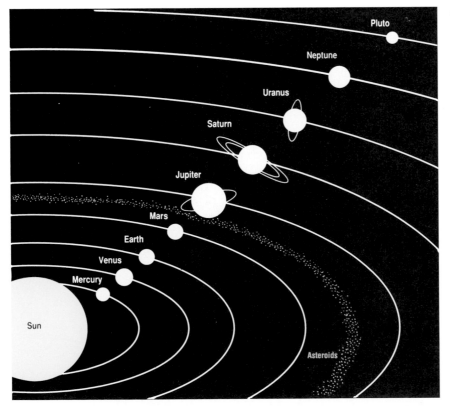

Asteroids at a glance

Asteroids, shown in orange in the diagram, occupy the space between Mars and Jupiter.

Distance from sun: Most asteroids are between the orbits of Mars (141.7 million miles, 228 million kilometers) and Jupiter (483.7 million miles, 778.4 million kilometers). Ceres, the largest asteroid, is at 257 million miles (414 million kilometers).

Number: at least 30,000. The orbits of over 3,000 are known.

Size: ranging from the largest, Ceres, about 600 miles (960 kilometers) in diameter, to less than 1 mile in diameter. About 30 asteroids have diameters greater than 120 miles (192 kilometers).

Shape: ranging from nearly ball-shaped to highly irregular.

Composition: mostly rock or a mixture of rock and metal.

69

are heavily cratered from billions of years of collisions with other objects.

Scientists think many asteroids have been broken into pieces by violent collisions with one another. In some cases, the fragments fell back together again, attracted by their own gravity, to form a cloud of rubble orbiting the sun. Other asteroids might have smaller asteroids orbiting around them. Still others might come in pairs that perhaps touch as they slowly rotate around each other.

Most asteroids are too small to be seen even with powerful optical telescopes. Yet, scientists have learned something about what asteroids are like by analyzing the light reflected off their surfaces. By breaking down the light with a device called a spectrograph, astronomers have found that asteroids have different surface compositions. Some are made of rock, and others are mixtures of rock and metal. A rare few even have lava plains on their surfaces, like the lunar maria.

METEORITES

Scientists may already have samples of asteroidal material, even though no spacecraft has ever visited an asteroid. These samples may be fragments blasted off the surface of asteroids during violent collisions. In such collisions, fragments of rock or metal—called meteoroids—shoot into space in all directions.

Some enter Earth's atmosphere, where friction with the air makes them glowing hot. We see them as bright streaks of light, called meteors or falling stars. Meteoroids that reach Earth's surface before burning up are called meteorites.

What do meteorites tell us about asteroids? Some meteorites, called chondrites, may be chunks of the original material that formed the sun and planets. Certain chondrites—called carbonaceous chondrites—contain organic molecules, the chemical building blocks of life, and are 4.6 billion years old—as old as the solar system itself. Phobos and Deimos, the two moons of Mars, are probably made of carbonaceous chondrite material.

ACTIVE ASTEROIDS

Not all asteroids have remained unchanged since their formation. Some became so hot inside that their interiors melted, forming metal cores and dense, rocky mantles like Earth's. Some of these asteroids must have been shattered to bits by collisions with other asteroids, because we have found meteorites made of iron or mixtures of iron and rock—samples of the cores and mantles of these fragmented asteroids.

Some scientists have proposed mining asteroids for their metals—even a small asteroid could supply many tons of metal for industries on Earth and in space.

Some meteorites are made of basalt, a volcanic rock also found on Earth and the moon. The asteroids that spawned these basaltic meteorites must have been volcanically active at some time in their history. On

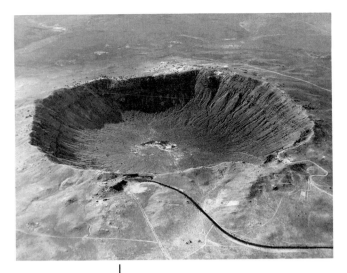

Some 50,000 years ago, a meteorite slammed into Earth and formed the Meteor Crater in northeastern Arizona. It is about 4,150 feet (1,265 meters) across and 570 feet (174 meters) deep.

On August 10, 1972, a meteor skipped through Earth's atmosphere and continued out into space. This picture of the meteor was taken in Grand Teton National Park in Wyoming.

these asteroids, molten rock erupted to the surface and formed lava plains. Some of the basaltic meteorites have tentatively been traced to Vesta, one of the largest asteroids.

ASTEROID EXPLORATION

Both the United States and the Soviet Union plan to send spacecraft to explore asteroids sometime around the end of this decade. Close-up pictures of an asteroid would tell much about the processes that have affected it since its formation. But most valuable of all would be a piece of an asteroid brought back to Earth for study. With pictures and other data on the asteroid it came from, scientists might learn more from the sample than from meteorites, whose origins are not known for certain. If asteroids really are the leftovers from the birth of the solar system, they may have much to tell us about how the solar system came to be.

Three of the four Galilean satellites are shown orbiting above Jupiter's multicolored clouds. The Great Red Spot can be seen on the lower left portion of the planet.

JUPITER

Jupiter—named for the king of the gods of ancient Rome—is the mightiest of planets in the solar system. It is the largest planet, some 88,700 miles (141,920 kilometers) across, more than 10 times the size of Earth. Jupiter is so big that if it were hollow, all the other planets would fit inside it.

Jupiter is more like the sun than like Earth. Like the sun, Jupiter is mostly hydrogen, with a small amount of helium. In addition, the clouds of Jupiter contain water, methane, ammonia, and other compounds of nitrogen, hydrogen, and sulfur, all of which are thought to have existed in the earliest atmosphere of Earth. Scientists think that if Jupiter had been about 70 times more massive, it would have been a star. As it is, Jupiter is something halfway between a star and a solid planet.

THE CLOUDS OF JUPITER

Through even a small telescope, Jupiter displays distinct light and dark bands that cross the planet parallel to its equator. Jupiter has no solid surface—these bands are clouds. The planet rotates so fast—once every 10 hours at the equator—that its clouds are drawn out into alternating light and dark bands, which astronomers call belts and zones. The belts and zones race around the planet at high speeds, like the jet streams in Earth's atmosphere.

It is difficult to see any detail in Jupiter's clouds, since at its closest the planet is some 391 million miles (626 million kilometers) from us. But spacecraft have flown past Jupiter and taken close-up pictures, which show that its turbulent clouds are constantly changing. The composition of the clouds is not definitely known, but they appear to be made up of three layers. The bottom layer may be composed of water in the form of ice crystals and possibly droplets of liquid water. The middle layer may contain a compound

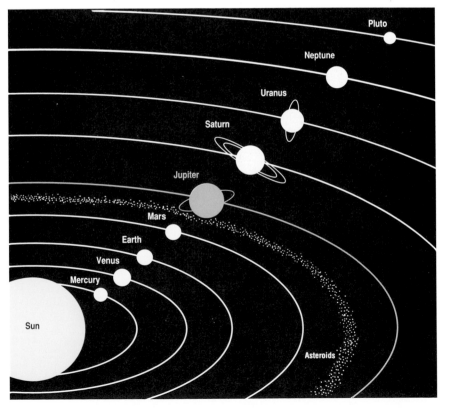

Jupiter at a glance

Jupiter, shown in orange in the diagram, is the fifth closest planet to the sun.

Distance from the sun: *Shortest*—460,000,000 miles (740,000,000 kilometers); *Greatest*—507,000,000 miles (816,000,000 kilometers); *Mean*—483,700,000 miles (778,400,000 kilometers).

Distance from the earth: *Shortest*—390,700,000 miles (628,760,000 kilometers); *Greatest*—600,000,000 miles (970,000,000 kilometers).

Diameter: 88,700 miles (141,920 kilometers).

Length of year: About 12 earth-years.

Rotation period: 9 hours and 55 minutes.

Average temperature: −236° F. (−149° C).

Atmosphere: Hydrogen, helium, methane, ammonia, carbon monoxide, ethane, acetylene, phosphine, water vapor.

Number of satellites: 16.

of ammonia and hydrogen sulfide, and the uppermost layer seems to be ammonia ice crystals.

Perhaps the most fascinating of Jupiter's features is the Great Red Spot, a gigantic storm three times the size of Earth that has been raging for at least a few hundred years. It has changed in appearance over the years, becoming very prominent at some times and nearly disappearing at others.

No one knows what has kept the Great Red Spot going for so long, but it may get its energy from the atmospheric jets around it, like a ball bearing spinning between two conveyor belts. Motion pictures made from *Voyager* spacecraft images show that the Great Red Spot spins counterclockwise, the same direction as hurricanes in Earth's Northern Hemisphere. Perhaps by studying the Great Red Spot, meteorologists will learn more about storms in our own atmosphere.

JUPITER'S RADIATION

Jupiter does something very strange: it radiates about twice as much heat as it receives from the sun. Scientists think the heat is still escaping from the time Jupiter was formed.

Most of the contraction occurred long ago. Early in its history, Jupiter probably glowed red hot. It would have been an awesome sight in the skies of its newly formed satellites. Today, Jupiter is probably still shrinking at a slow rate that is too small to measure.

Jupiter's clouds are very cold, about $-236°$ F. ($-149°$ C). But deep within the planet's interior, temperatures may rise to thousands of degrees above zero. Somewhere between the extremes, perhaps below the visible clouds, the temperatures

This photograph of Jupiter's Great Red Spot was taken by Voyager 2 in July, 1979. This photo is different from the one taken of the same region by Voyager 1, showing that the dense layer of clouds around Jupiter is constantly changing.

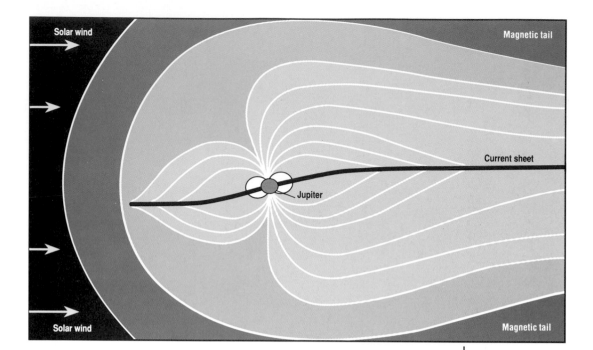

Solar wind

Magnetic tail

Current sheet

Jupiter

Solar wind

Magnetic tail

Jupiter's invisible magnetosphere is many times larger than the planet itself. The magnetosphere is molded by the solar wind into a magnetic tail that stretches away from the sun. The current sheet is a thin band of electrically charged particles.

may be similar to those found over the surface of Earth and would be comfortable for life as we know it. It has been suggested that perhaps a form of life exists there, floating within the lower atmosphere.

Some scientists believe Jupiter's extra heat is the energy source for the planet's swirling clouds. Others say Jupiter's clouds, like Earth's, get their energy from sunlight. To resolve the question, scientists are eagerly awaiting the unmanned *Galileo* spacecraft's mission to Jupiter in the early 1990's.

Besides heat, Jupiter's magnetosphere traps high-energy particles, such as hydrogen, helium, oxygen, and sulfur ions. These particles form belts of intense radiation in Jupiter's magnetic field.

INSIDE AND OUTSIDE JUPITER

No one knows what the interior of Jupiter is like. Beneath the clouds, perhaps 600 miles (960 kilometers) down, there may be a layer of hydrogen in liquid form, due to the intense pressures and low temperatures. Deeper in the interior, pressures may squeeze the liquid hydrogen so much that it behaves more like metal than liquid. Finally, there might be a solid core roughly the size of Earth at Jupiter's center, composed of iron and other metals and rock.

When the *Voyager 1* spacecraft flew past Jupiter in 1979, it discovered that the planet is encircled by a thin ring like Saturn's, only much smaller, roughly 4,000 miles (6,400 kilometers) wide. The ring is made of microscopic, dark particles of unknown origin.

This mosaic of four photographs taken by Voyager 2 *clearly* shows the thin ring around Jupiter. Because the space probe was on Jupiter's nightside when the picture was taken, the sun outlined the planet's shape with a bright halo.

In this multiple-exposure photograph taken by Voyager 1, *Jupiter's extremely thin ring appears as a broad, light band crossing the center of the picture. The background stars look like broken hairpins because of spacecraft motion during the time exposure. The black dots are calibration points in the camera.*

When Galileo turned his telescope on Jupiter in 1610, he discovered that the planet has four large satellites. Today, astronomers know that at least 16 moons orbit Jupiter, forming a kind of miniature solar system. These satellites probably condensed out of a cloud of gas and dust orbiting Jupiter, just as the planets condensed out of a similar cloud surrounding the sun. Jupiter's cloud contained some dust and a great deal of water; today, its satellites are mixtures of rock and ice. Most of the satellites are small, insignificant chunks about which little is known. But Galileo's four discoveries—called the Galilean satellites—are fascinating worlds, small planets in their own right.

Callisto

The outermost of the Galilean satellites, Callisto, is a ball of ice and rock some 3,000 miles (4,800 kilometers) across, making it about the same size as the planet Mercury. Callisto's entire surface is covered with impact craters. Billions of years of bombardment by cosmic debris are visible on its dark, icy crust. Some of Callisto's craters are surrounded by bright rays of ice blasted out of subsurface layers. There is a huge, ringed impact basin called Valhalla, possibly the largest impact crater in the solar system. Researchers believe Callisto's icy crust flowed very slowly, smoothing out major topographic features over billions of years. Valhalla and other large craters on Callisto have flattened out completely, leaving only light colored circular patches.

Ganymede

Moving inward from Callisto, we encounter Ganymede, the largest moon in the solar system. Its diameter is approximately 3,300 miles (5,300 kilometers). Like Callisto, Ganymede is probably half frozen water and half rock.

Seen from a great distance, Ganymede displays dark patches set against a light background. Close-up photographs show that the dark areas resemble Callisto's heavily cratered surface. But the dark areas on Ganymede are surrounded by lighter colored terrain, crisscrossed by peculiar ridges and grooves. The grooves seem to be places where Ganymede's crust was fractured, allowing water to pour out from the interior.

Ganymede's grooved terrain— where blocks of ice have slid past each other—reminds scientists of Earth's crustal plates. Although the grooves are younger than Ganymede's dark areas, they are still very old, having formed perhaps 4 billion years ago. At that time, Jupiter is thought to have been much brighter and hotter than today. It probably glowed red hot. Ganymede, being closer than Callisto, felt the effects of Jupiter's heat more. As Jupiter cooled down, Ganymede's geologic activity slowly ceased.

Europa

The next moon in from Ganymede is Europa, 1,945 miles (3,112 kilometers) across. Europa contains a lower percentage of water than Ganymede and Callisto. This might be because Eu-

Jupiter's four Galilean moons are also the four largest of the planet's 16 known satellites: Io (upper left); *Europa* (upper right); *Ganymede* (lower left); *and Callisto* (lower right).

This photograph shows a special color reconstruction of one of the erupting volcanoes on Io discovered by Voyager 1.

ropa formed closer to Jupiter, where temperatures were higher and less water condensed.

Europa's icy surface is one of the brightest in the solar system. Strangely, the satellite is as smooth as a billiard ball—no large impact craters, mountains, or major relief of any kind has been found on its surface. It is likely that water has flowed onto the surface and frozen, covering everything with a smooth sheet of bright, fresh ice.

Europa is covered by a network of dark and light lines. Geologists think that at some time in Europa's history the crust cracked, in the same manner that sea ice on Earth does. Later, presumably, the cracks were filled in by water or other material from below, which froze and created the dark and light lines that we see today.

No one can say what lies beneath the icy crust of Europa, but there may be a deep ocean of water or slushy ice. What would keep this ocean from freezing? Scientists think massive Jupiter and the other Galilean satellites may constantly tug at Europa, causing it to flex. Such gravitational tuggings may have heated Europa's interior, melting some of its ice and creating a subterranean ocean. Some scientists have proposed that some form of life might be found in such an ocean if it exists. Most of Europa, however, is probably made of rocky material.

Io

Io, the innermost of the four Galilean satellites, is a bizzarre world about the size of Earth's moon. But it is nothing like the moon or any other planet. Instead of ice, Io is mostly rock. Heat from the infant Jupiter might have been enough to keep any water from condensing when this nearby moon formed.

Io is covered with active volcanoes. These volcanoes, according to many scientists, pour forth primarily molten sulfur. Io's volcanoes also spray umbrella-shaped plumes of sulfur dioxide ice crystals up to 200 miles (320 kilometers) or more into space, giving the satellite a thin sulfur dioxide atmosphere.

Io's surface is very cold, about −231° F. (−146° C), but at the mouths of its volcanoes, temperatures as high as 63° F. (17° C) have been recorded. Sulfur that pours out of the volcanoes onto Io's surface quickly solidifies in the cold of space.

When the *Voyager 1* spacecraft flew by Io in 1979, eight volcanoes were erupting at once. By comparison, no more than one or two volcanoes are likely to be erupting at any one time on Earth. Io is easily the most active world geologically in the solar system.

What powers Io's volcanoes? Io experiences strong tidal stresses caused by the gravitational forces of Jupiter and other moons, especially Europa. These tidal forces squeeze and unsqueeze Io in each orbit. Such flexing pumps energy into the interior of Io in the form of heat. As a result, widespread and recurrent volcanic eruptions occur.

Io's volcanoes pour out so much material that the surface of this moon is constantly changing. In fact, one could say that Io is continually turning itself inside out. No impact craters of any kind have been spotted on Io. They must lie buried deep beneath Io's present surface.

You would not want to go to Io without all kinds of protective gear. Apart from the extreme cold, Io orbits inside the deadly radiation belts associated with Jupiter's magnetic field. But if you could somehow safely visit this sulfurous moon, you would behold an awesome sight—Jupiter, as seen from Io, appears some 40 times larger than our moon looks from Earth. For the time being, however, scientists will probably send unmanned spacecraft to explore Io's fantastic surface.

Captured Asteroids?

Little is known of Jupiter's 12 other moons. Four small bodies circle Jupiter inside Io's orbit. The largest of these is Amalthea, a potato-shaped moon probably made of rock. Amalthea has a reddish surface that may be coated with sulfur. Two other groups of moons orbit beyond Callisto. Four are located about 7,000,000 miles (11,200,000 kilometers) from Jupiter, and another 4 are about 14,000,000 miles (22,400,000 kilometers) out. This last group circles Jupiter in the opposite direction compared to the other 12 satellites. And all 8 of these outer moons have orbits that are highly inclined to Jupiter's equator. They may be asteroids captured by Jupiter's gravity, or they may be fragments of larger moons that broke apart.

Scientists will learn more about Jupiter and its miniature solar system when the *Galileo* spacecraft arrives in the early 1990's.

SATURN

Because of its majestic system of rings, Saturn has earned a place as one of the most beautiful planets in the solar system. Even a small telescope will show the rings surrounding the tan colored ball of Saturn itself. What are these rings? In a telescope, they look like solid sheets, but they are actually composed of billions of particles orbiting Saturn. The perimeter of the outer- most ring may measure up to 272,400 miles (435,800 kilometers). It extends outward from Saturn as far as 46,000 miles (74,000 kilometers). All the rings are relatively thin, varying in thickness from about 660 feet (198 meters) to 9,800 feet (2,940 meters).

Most of the ring particles range in size from small chunks only an inch or so across to boulders the size of a house. The ring particles are apparently snowballs made of ice, but there may be other matter, such as dust, hidden inside them.

THE RINGS OF SATURN

There are seven major parts to the rings around Saturn. From Earth, astronomers can see three main parts of the rings that are called, from outermost to innermost, ring A, ring B, and ring C. Of these, A is fairly dark, B is the brightest, and C is semitransparent and more difficult to see. A fourth ring, called ring D, is too faint to be seen from Earth; it lies inside ring C. Rings F, G, and E lie outside ring A.

When the *Voyager 1* spacecraft sent back close-up pictures of Saturn in 1980, astronomers were amazed to find that each of the major rings is composed of thousands of narrow ringlets, or bands, giving the appearance of grooves on a phonograph record. *Voyager 1* also observed several narrow rings outside ring A. All in all, Saturn's ringlets probably number in the thousands.

A 3,100-mile (4,960-kilometer) gap, called the Cassini division, separates ring A from ring B. In addition, there is a gap within the A ring called the Encke division, also named the Keeler gap. Numerous small gaps exist throughout Saturn's rings.

BIZARRE DISCOVERIES

Most of the rings follow simple, nearly circular paths around Saturn. But a few are quite peculiar. Some rings are elliptical compared to the rest. Others have wavy edges. But the strangest

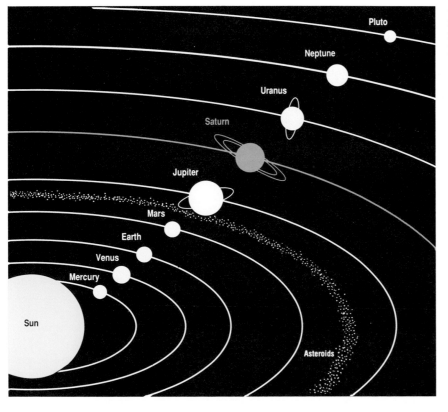

Saturn at a glance

Saturn, shown in orange in the diagram, is the sixth closest planet to the sun.

83

Distance from sun: *Shortest*—838,000,000 mi. (1,349,000,000 km); *Greatest*—932,000,000 mi. (1,500,000,000 km); *Mean*—885,200,000 mi. (1,424,600,000 km).

Distance from earth: *Shortest*—762,700,000 mi. (1,277,400,000 km); *Greatest*—1,030,000,000 mi. (1,658,000,000 km).

Diameter: About 74,600 mi. (120,000 km).

Length of year: About 29.5 earth-years.

Rotation period: 10 hours 39 minutes.

Temperature: −285° F. (−176° C).

Atmosphere: Hydrogen, helium, methane, ammonia, ethane, and phosphine (?).

Number of satellites: 23.

An artist's conception of the view from within Saturn's rings shows chunks of ice in various sizes. The orange sphere to the left is Saturn, and the bright light to the right is the sun.

Giovanni Domenico Cassini (1625–1712), the Italian-born French astronomer, was the first director of the Paris Observatory. His achievements include the discovery of four of Saturn's moons and the detection of a gap between two rings, which now bears his name: the Cassini division.

ring is F, photographed by the Voyager probes. This ring appears to be made of several separate strands, each less than 16 miles (25 kilometers) wide, that seem to be braided around each other. Scientists are mystified by ring F's strange braids, which cannot be explained by the normal laws of orbital motion.

Voyager 1 found two small moons circling Saturn on either side of ring F. Their gravitational attraction for particles keeps the ring confined to a narrow band. Perhaps the moons also create a gravitational disturbance in the ring's strands, causing their mysterious distortions. Scientists named the two moons the shepherding satellites. Another tiny moon orbits just outside ring A, and it appears to keep the ring's edge sharply defined.

Saturn's major satellites are far away from the edge of the rings, but they also influence the ring's particles with their gravity. Scientists are only beginning to understand the complex effects the moons have on the rings. The moons may be responsible for creating gaps in the rings, such as the Cassini and Encke divisions.

A final ring mystery, also photographed by *Voyager 1*, is dusky shadings that cross ring B like spokes on a wheel. The spokes travel around Saturn with the ring, changing in size and brightness as they continually emerge

This color-enhanced photograph showing a section of Saturn's rings was taken by Voyager 2 in August, 1981. The rings can be seen to consist of thousands of thin ringlets.

This photograph was taken by Voyager 2 in August, 1981. It shows sporadically spaced "spokes" in the outer half of the broad B ring.

and fade away. As with so many features of Saturn's rings, these spokes are difficult to explain. One theory says they are made of particles that are held floating above the ring by electric forces and are swept along in Saturn's magnetic field as the planet rotates.

Astronomers are still trying to find out how Saturn's rings came to be. They know that the rings are located inside Saturn's Roche limit, which is the point at which Saturn's gravity would break apart a large, weak object. The ring particles may have condensed from the same cloud of gas and dust that formed Saturn and its moons. Because they are inside Saturn's Roche limit, they never became joined into a single body. Or, they may be the remains of a body that broke apart after straying inside the Roche limit.

JUPITER'S FIRST COUSIN

What of Saturn itself? Like Jupiter, it is made of hydrogen and a small amount of helium. But Saturn is less dense than Jupiter. Its density is less than that of water, which means that if there were an ocean enormous enough to put Saturn in, the planet would float.

Cassini division

Ring B

Ring C

Ring A

Enke division

Pioneer division

This cutaway view of Saturn shows what the interior is thought to be like. It also shows the major ring features surrounding the planet.

Outer core of ammonia, methane, and water

Liquid molecular hydrogen and helium

Liquid metallic hydrogen

Inner iron-rich core

Ring D

This color-enhanced image of Saturn's clouds shows light and dark bands that move rapidly around the planet. The swirling features within the bands may be atmospheric storms.

Christian Huygens (1629–1695), a Dutch mathematician, physicist, and astronomer, was the first person to see and describe the rings around Saturn. He also discovered the first known Saturnian moon, Titan.

Saturn is twice as far from the sun as Jupiter is. Temperatures at Saturn's cloud-tops average a frigid −285° F. (−176° C). Saturn's clouds are arranged in light and dark bands like Jupiter's, but they are less distinct. In part, this is because Saturn's clouds are shrouded by a high-altitude haze of ice crystals.

Saturn's cloud bands are fewer in number than Jupiter's, but they move faster—more than 1,000 miles (1,600 kilometers) per hour along the equator. Saturn also has oval-shaped features that are probably giant storms. Saturn's clouds, like Jupiter's, are arranged in layers of different composition that may be composed of water, ammonia and hydrogen sulfide, and ammonia ice crystals.

Saturn also radiates far more heat than it receives from the sun—up to two and one-half times as much. Presumably, this heat is the energy source for Saturn's swift winds. But without sending a spacecraft to study Saturn in more detail, scientists cannot be sure.

SATURN'S FAMILY OF SATELLITES

Like Jupiter, Saturn and its satellites are like a miniature solar system. Saturn has at least 23 known moons, more than any other planet. Compared to Jupiter's moons, most of Saturn's satellites are composed mainly of frozen water. When the Voyager probes flew by Saturn, scientists expected to see a repeat of the pattern they had found in Jupiter's Galilean satellites: the farther a moon was from the planet when it formed, the less dense it would be, containing presumably more water. But no such pattern seems to exist among Saturn's moons. The Saturnian satellites vary in density and composition with seeming randomness.

We've already learned that one moon orbits just beyond ring A's outer edge, and that two moons flank ring F. Two more are found roughly halfway between rings F and G. These two moonlets share nearly the same orbit, so scientists call them the co-orbital satellites. The larger of the two measures 100 by 140 miles (160 by 224 kilometers).

Mimas

Mimas is the innermost of Saturn's major satellites. It is a small iceball, only 240 miles (384 kilometers) across. Mimas is covered with craters, and in close-up pictures it looks like an icy version of the moon or Mercury. One enormous crater is 80 miles (128 kilometers) in diameter, one-third the size of the satellite. It looks like a giant eye staring out from one side of the tiny moon. The impact that formed this crater must have come close to shattering Mimas to bits.

Seen from Mimas, Saturn is 70 times bigger than the full moon seen from Earth. Because Mimas always keeps the same face turned to the planet, Saturn never sets in Mimas' sky. If you stood on Mimas for one complete orbit around Saturn (taking only 23 hours), you would see the giant planet go through phases from full to crescent to new, and back to full again.

Enceladus

Moving out from Mimas, we encounter another small, icy moon called Enceladus. Like Jupiter's satellite Ganymede, Enceladus displays different types of surface features. Parts of Enceladus are cratered, but some areas have no craters at all. Instead, they are covered by smooth, fresh ice like the surface of Europa, another moon of Jupiter. Researchers think water volcanism—in which water rather than lava flows onto the surface from the interior—has resurfaced the smooth areas of Enceladus. As with Jupiter's moon Io, the heat for Enceladus' volcanoes probably comes from the gravitational tugs of Saturn and other moons, which flex Enceladus' interior. Active water volcanoes may exist there today.

Scientists think of Enceladus as a world intermediate in character between Jupiter's moons Europa and Ganymede. Why didn't Mimas, which is about the same size as Enceladus, turn out the same way? This is only one of many unanswered questions scientists have about Saturn's family of satellites.

Tethys

Tethys is the next Saturnian moon, and it closely resembles Mimas. Like Mimas, Tethys has a large impact crater that dominates one side of the moon. Tethys also has a huge canyon, called *Ithaca Chasma*, that stretches three-quarters of the way around the satellite. Tethys shares its orbit with two tiny moons. Like the Trojan asteroids that share Jupiter's orbit, these two bodies orbit 60 degrees ahead of and behind Tethys.

Dione and Rhea

Next come two similar, icy moons, Dione and Rhea. Both are heavily cratered, and both always keep the same face turned toward Saturn. Like Tethys, Dione is accompanied by a small moonlet orbiting 60 degrees ahead of it.

Dione and Rhea each display mysterious, bright streaks on one side, the side that trails each moon as they orbit Saturn. The origin of these streaks is not known, but they may be fractures in the moons' crusts that are lined with bright frost.

Mysterious Titan

Titan, located 759,000 miles (1,213,400 kilometers) from Saturn, is perhaps the most intriguing of all the Saturnian satellites. It is a planet-sized body, about 3,200 miles (5,120 kilometers) across. When the Voyagers flew past Titan, scientists who hoped to get a glimpse of its surface were disappointed. They found that Titan is completely hidden by a blanket of smog—organic compounds produced by the effect of sunlight on the methane in Titan's atmosphere. Other data showed that Titan's atmosphere is mostly nitrogen. The atmosphere is quite dense, and even though Titan is less than half the size of Earth, the pressure at Titan's surface is about 1.6 times greater than that at the surface of our own planet.

A thick layer of smog completely envelops Titan, Saturn's largest satellite. The upper level of the smog is seen here as an orange haze. Titan is one of the few satellites in the solar system known to have an atmosphere.

Scientists are especially interested in Titan's atmosphere because it contains organic molecules like ethane, acetylene, ethylene, and hydrogen cyanide. Life on Earth is thought to have evolved from such organic building blocks. In this respect, Titan may be like the primitive Earth, but it is certainly far colder, about −292° F. (−180° C).

What might Titan's surface be like? The surface, once thought to be made of frozen water, is now believed to be a mixture of frozen and liquid methane nearly one-half mile (0.8 kilometer) deep. Rocks of frozen ammonia and water may also be present. Organic molecules, like methane, are thought to rain down like droplets of tar from the thick smog above. What a bizarre world Titan might be.

The Strange Outer Moons

Each of Saturn's outermost satellites is strange and mysterious. Hyperion, orbiting 933,000 miles (1,492,800 kilometers) from Saturn, is a hamburger-shaped chunk measuring about 125 miles (200 kilometers) in length, 80 miles (128 kilometers) in width, and 60 miles (96 kilometers) in depth. Its composition is unknown, but it may be icy like the other Saturnian moons. Hyperion's unusual shape makes some scientists think it is a fragment of a larger body that was destroyed by collision with an asteroid.

Iapetus, the next moon out, is truly puzzling. One side of Iapetus—the side that trails the moon as it goes around Saturn—is covered with bright ice. The other side is dark as asphalt. What could account for this strange appearance? Some scientists have proposed that the dark side is coated with a layer of carbon-filled dust, similar to chondrite meteorites that may have derived from Phoebe, the outermost Saturnian moon.

Phoebe appears to be made of dark material like that on Iapetus' dark, leading hemisphere. Perhaps impacts on Phoebe have blasted material into space. Eventually, researchers suggest, some of this dust was swept up by Iapetus. But such an explanation does not account for the fact that some of Iapetus' dark material seems to have come from its interior. Until another spacecraft visits Iapetus to investigate, the mystery of its two-faced appearance may remain unsolved.

Phoebe itself is another oddball moon. It moves retrograde, or backward, in a highly elliptical orbit that is inclined by 30 degrees to Saturn's equator. With its dark, carbon-covered surface, Phoebe doesn't seem to belong with the rest of Saturn's satellites. Scientists have suggested that Phoebe may be an asteroid that was captured by Saturn's gravity.

Saturn, its rings, and its family of satellites are still in many ways mysterious to astronomers. The more we know of this fascinating miniature solar system, the more questions seem to arise. Scientists anxiously await future missions to Saturn to help answer the growing list of questions.

Mimas, one of Saturn's icy moons, reveals a huge impact crater in this image taken by Voyager 1. The central icy peak of the crater rises about 6 miles (10 kilometers) above the floor, higher than Mount Everest.

URANUS

This composite picture of Uranus, its rings, and its moon Miranda was made from photographs taken by **Voyager 2** in 1986.

More than 600 million miles (1 billion kilometers) beyond Saturn, we find the seventh planet, Uranus. It was the first planet discovered after prehistoric times. Like Jupiter and Saturn, it is a giant, gaseous world. But it is smaller and far less massive. Uranus had only 5 percent of Jupiter's mass, but has 92 percent of its density. It has about 15 percent of Saturn's mass, but is about 3 times as dense. These differences suggest that Uranus is very different in composition than its giant sunward neighbors.

In an optical telescope, Uranus is a small, greenish dot. The green color results from absorption of red light by methane in Uranus' cloud layers. About 60 to 90 miles (96 to 144 kilometers) below Uranus' cloud tops, a mixture of water, methane, ammonia, hydrogen, and helium forms a thick, oceanlike layer of liquid. This probably forms the bulk of Uranus.

Voyager 2's discovery of a substantial magnetic field surrounding Uranus implies that the planet possesses a small molten core. Also, unlike Jupiter and Saturn, Uranus does not seem to be radiating excess heat.

Uranus orbits the sun on its side, making one complete revolution in 84 earth-years. This means that seasons and days on Uranus are very different from ours on Earth. While the planet's north pole is facing the sun, as it is today, the northern (summer) hemisphere is in daylight while the southern (winter) hemisphere is perpetually in darkness. Twenty-one years from now, when it is autumn in the northern hemisphere, the sun will shine directly over Uranus' equator, and a day will equal one rotation of the planet on its axis. Then comes 21 years of summer and daytime in the southern hemisphere, then a 21-year southern autumn, and so on. Scientists have no explanation for Uranus' sideways tilt. Perhaps early in its history, the planet was struck by a large body, knocking it into its present orientation.

Uranus has 15 moons, all orbiting in the plane of the planet's equator. The Uranian moons probably range in the size of their diameters from about 10 to 990 miles (15 to 1,590 kilometers). It has been difficult for astronomers to learn much about these satellites. However, it is believed that they are composed of rock and ice.

In 1977, astronomers discovered that Uranus is encircled by nine dark rings. When Uranus passed in front of a distant star, the rings caused momentary "blinks" in the star's light before and after the planet itself passed in front of the star. In early 1986, *Voyager 2* discovered an additional two rings, bringing the total number of known rings to eleven. Astronomers believe there are many more rings yet to be discovered. The rings are not icy like Saturn's. Instead, they appear to be made of small, dark particles.

Uranus, its rings, and satellites are still largely unknown, despite the close-up pictures and other data provided by *Voyager 2* in 1986. Further exploration should provide more interesting information on the seventh planet.

Four of the fifteen moons of Uranus, all in the plane of the planet's equator, are shown orbiting the planet in these pictures. The overexposure brings the moons into focus, but distorts the image of Uranus. Because the planet's north pole currently faces the sun, the moons are seen from the "top," rather than from the "side," in which case they would all be along an imaginary line going from left to right.

Uranus at a glance

Uranus, shown in orange in the diagram, is the seventh closest planet to the sun.

Distance from sun: *Shortest—* 1,700,000,000 mi. (2,720,000,000 km); *Greatest—*1,860,000,000 mi. (2,999,000,000 km); *Mean—* 1,781,000,000 mi. (2,866,900,000 km).

Distance from earth: *Shortest—* 1,700,000,000 mi. (2,720,000,000 km); *Greatest—*1,960,000,000 mi. (3,154,000,000 km).

Diameter: 31,570 mi. (50,800 km).

Length of year: 30,685 earth-days.

Rotation period: 17 hours.

Temperature: $-357°$ F. $(-216°$ C).

Atmosphere: Hydrogen, helium, methane, acetylene.

Number of satellites: 15.

An artist's conception
of what Neptune might
look like from its
moon Triton.

NEPTUNE

After Uranus was discovered in
1781, astronomers began to notice that its path around the sun
did not conform to Kepler's laws
of motion, which mathemati-
cally describe planetary orbits.
The astronomers reasoned that
perhaps some unknown planet
lay beyond Uranus and was af-
fecting Uranus' orbit with its
gravitational pull.

In 1846, astronomers found
Neptune, which lies some 2.8
billion miles (4.5 billion kilometers) from the sun—30 times farther than Earth. As it turns out,
Neptune's gravity does not account for Uranus' motion. As-

Neptune's two moons
are indicated by the
arrows in this photo-
graph. Triton is clos-
est to Neptune, while
Nereid is much farther
away.

Urbain J. J. Leverrier (1811–1877) was a French mathematician who correctly predicted the mass, orbit, and position of Neptune solely from its gravitational effect on Uranus.

tronomers still don't understand the cause.

At first glance, Neptune seems to be a twin of Uranus. Both planets are about the same size and possess thick, dense atmospheres of hydrogen and methane gas, along with some helium. Neptune's clouds, however, are often topped by a layer of ice crystals, while Uranus is usually free of such icy haze. Most importantly, Neptune is slightly more dense than Uranus, and it radiates excess heat while Uranus does not.

From the little they know about Neptune, astronomers think it may have a solid, highly compressed rocky core surrounded by a thick layer of ice in which excess heat travels to the surface by convection, the same process that aids in the outward radiation of the sun's energy. Unlike Uranus, no magnetic field has been detected.

Neptune has two unusual satellites: Nereid and Triton. Nereid follows a long, narrow, elliptical orbit that is inclined to Neptune's equator. Triton's orbit is circular, but also highly inclined. And Triton moves in a retrograde direction—opposite to Neptune's rotation. Recently, astronomers detected methane frost on Triton's surface and found that it may have an ocean of liquid nitrogen.

Neptune, like Uranus, is shrouded in mystery. Scientists are eagerly awaiting *Voyager 2*'s encounter with the planet and its moons in 1989. Does Neptune, like the other three gas giant planets Jupiter, Saturn, and Uranus, possess a system of rings? Conflicting evidence has been obtained over the last few years, but *Voyager 2* should resolve that question once and for all.

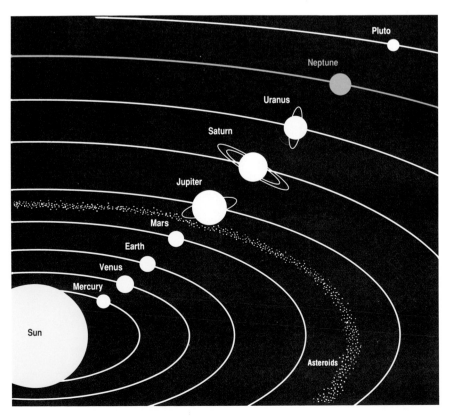

Neptune at a glance

Neptune, shown in orange in the diagram, is the eighth planet out from the sun.

Distance from sun: *Shortest*—2,754,000,000 mi. (4,432,500,000 km); *Greatest*—2,832,000,000 mi. (4,539,800,000 km); *Mean*—2,788,000,000 mi. (4,486,100,000 km).

Distance from earth: *Shortest*—2,700,000,000 mi. (4,350,000,000 km); *Greatest*—2,750,000,000 mi. (4,426,000,000 km).

Diameter: 30,200 mi. (48,600 km).

Length of year: About 165 earth-years.

Rotation period: About 16 hours.

Temperature: $-360°$ F. ($-218°$ C).

Atmosphere: Hydrogen, helium, methane, and ethane(?).

Number of satellites: Two.

PLUTO

Pluto is named for the ancient Roman god of the underworld. Averaging some 3.6 billion miles (5.8 billion kilometers) from the sun, Pluto moves in a realm of near darkness and extreme cold—temperatures at Pluto's surface hover around −369° F. (−223° C). From Pluto's surface, the sun would be a large, bright dot set against the backdrop of other stars.

Pluto was discovered in 1930 by Clyde Tombaugh, ending a search that was begun 25 years earlier by Percival Lowell. Lowell had begun looking for a *Planet X* when Neptune failed to account for the motion of Uranus. Pluto follows an inclined path around the sun that is so elliptical that it brings the planet inside the orbit of Neptune. Pluto crossed the orbit of Neptune in 1979 and will not regain its status as outermost planet until 1999.

Pluto is only a faint smudge in the largest telescopes. Its size, mass, and composition are not known with certainty. From the evidence that exists, astronomers believe Pluto is a body of ice and rock, less than a quarter the size of Earth. Several satellites of other planets are bigger than Pluto. Scientists have found evidence of methane frost and

An artist's conception of what Pluto's moon, Charon, might look like when viewed from Pluto's surface.

This magnified photograph of Pluto, taken in 1978, shows an apparent bulge in the planet. Astronomer James Christy concluded that the bulge was actually a moon, which has been named Charon.

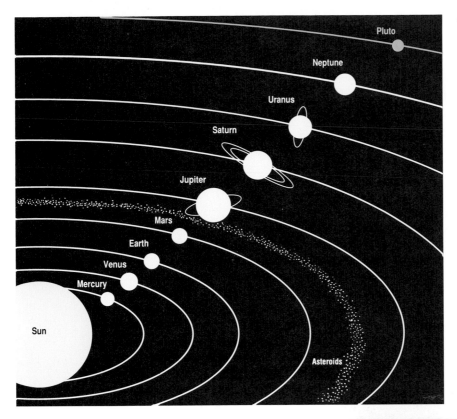

Pluto, shown in orange in the diagram, is the farthest planet from the sun.

Distance from the sun: *Shortest*—2,748,000,000 miles (4,423,200,000 kilometers); *Greatest*—4,571,200,000 miles (7,356,000,000 kilometers); *Mean*—3,660,000,000 miles (5,890,000,000 kilometers).

Distance from the earth: *Shortest*—3,583,000,000 miles (5,765,500,000 kilometers); *Greatest*—4,670,000,000 miles (7,516,000,000 kilometers).

Diameter: 1,900 miles (3,000 kilometers).

Length of year: About 248 earth-years.

Rotation period: About 6 earth-days.

Temperature: About $-342°$ to $-369°$ F. ($-208°$ to $-223°$ C).

Atmosphere: Methane.

Satellites: 1.

Even through powerful telescopes, Pluto looks like a dim star. Yet, these two photographs, taken a day apart, show Pluto's movement against the backdrop of distant stars.

indications of a methane atmosphere on Pluto, giving it a similarity to Neptune's moon Triton.

In 1978, astronomer James Christy discovered a small satellite orbiting Pluto. The moon has been given the name Charon, after the mythical ferryman who transports souls across the river Styx to the underworld. Charon is estimated to be about half the size of Pluto, making it the largest moon compared to its planet in the solar system. Pluto and Charon are sometimes called a double planet.

Charon is now helping astronomers to study Pluto. In 1985, Charon began to pass in front of Pluto, as seen from Earth, once each orbit. These periodic eclipses will last about five years. By analyzing the changing brightness of Pluto and Charon as they alternately pass in front of one another, as well as passing in and out of each other's shadows, astronomers hope to refine their estimates of the diameters, masses, and compositions of these two bodies.

With conventional rocket power, a direct flight to Pluto would take at least 10 years, probably more. No space missions are planned to Pluto in the near future. The mutual eclipses of Pluto and Charon should yield much new information, but scientists will probably have to wait until the 21st century for a close-up look.

Comet Bennett streaks across the sky above the Swiss Alps in 1970. It is estimated that this comet takes 1,680 years to orbit the sun.

COMETS

From the earliest times, comets have awed humanity with their brief appearances in the night sky, often accompanied by long, majestic tails stretching across the heavens. More often than not, comets were objects of fear. Many people believed they were evil omens. There was terror even in 1910, when the most famous comet of all—Halley's Comet—made an appearance.

In 1986 Halley's Comet again made its closest approach to Earth. In March of that year, unmanned spacecraft drew near to the comet, took close-up pictures, and gathered information on the comet's composition, structure, and activity.

DISTANT WANDERERS

For the majority of their lives, most comets roam in frigid darkness beyond Pluto, near the edges of the solar system. There may be as many as 200 billion comets circling the sun in a vast, spherical swarm called the

Oort Cloud. Occasionally, the gravity of a passing star flings a comet from its distant orbit to a new path in the inner solar system.

The majority of the approximately 700 comets discovered so far are long-period comets. These follow long, highly elliptical paths and take between hundreds and millions of years to complete one orbit of the sun. Over long periods of time, the gravitational tugs of massive Jupiter and other planets may change a comet's path into a more circular one. Such short-period comets complete one revolution of the sun in anything from years to a century or two. Halley's Comet is a short-period comet, since it makes one circuit approximately every 77 years. Its namesake, Edmond Halley, was the first to realize that comets can return on regular visits.

THE STRUCTURE OF A COMET

What is a comet? A comet is composed of two parts, a nucleus, or body, and a tail.

Resembling a dirty snowball, the nucleus consists of frozen gases, dust, and ice. It is an inactive chunk when far from the sun. No one has ever seen the nucleus of a comet, but some scientists think they are irregular lumps 6 miles (10 kilometers) or less in size.

When the nucleus approaches the sun, the sun's warming rays begin to cause its outer, icy layers to evaporate, releasing dust and gases. These form into a cloud, called a coma, around the nucleus.

As the comet heads for its rendezvous with the sun, sunlight exerts a minute pressure on the dust, while the gas molecules become caught up in the stream

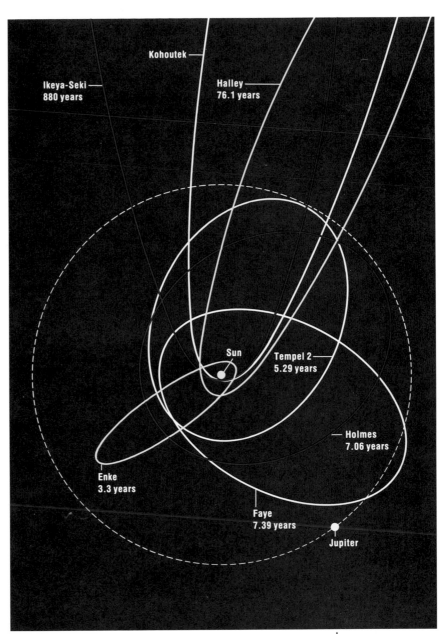

99

of charged particles known as the solar wind, which emanates from the sun. As a result, the gas and dust form into one or more tails, always pointing away from the sun.

A comet has no light source of its own. All its light is reflected sunlight. As such, it becomes brighter the closer it comes to perihelion, which is the point on its orbit closest to the sun.

Comets are often most spectacular just after perihelion, when the tails reach their great-

Comets orbit the sun in a wide variety of patterns and lengths of time. Some short-period comets, such as Enke, Holmes, and Tempel 2, travel within the orbit of Jupiter. Certain long-period comets, such as Kohoutek, are never expected to return to the inner solar system.

This is one of the first photographs ever taken of Halley's comet. It shows the famous comet as it appeared in 1910 passing near Earth.

100

est length. But there are no rules—comets are almost completely unpredictable. A comet may be spectacular on one visit and unimpressive on the next. They are subject to sudden changes in brightness. Some comets disappear altogether when their supply of ice is used up.

Once the comet rounds the sun, its activity slowly ceases. The nucleus heads for the outer reaches of the solar system, millions or perhaps many billions of miles (kilometers) from the sun, before it returns for another visit.

THE ORIGIN OF COMETS

Some astronomers believe comets were among the first things to condense from the cloud of gas and dust that spawned the sun and planets. Comets may have escaped the intense heating that wiped out the earliest history of the planets and their satellites. If so, comets could contain a record of the birth of the solar system. For that reason,

scientists are anxious to learn more about them. A spacecraft mission to rendezvous with a comet is being planned for the 1990's, and missions to obtain a sample of cometary material and bring it to Earth are on the drawing boards.

In the meantime, scientists think they may already have microscopic bits of cometary dust in their laboratories. Cosmic dust, which falls into Earth's upper atmosphere every day, is thought to be shed by comets during their visits. Scientists have used high-flying research planes to collect cosmic dust samples for analysis. Each grain is only a few microns (millionths of a meter) across and weighs only a billionth of a gram. Hence, the grains are extremely difficult to study.

Under a powerful electron microscope, many cosmic dust grains turn out to be collections of much smaller grains joined together. This is precisely the structure scientists expect a comet to have—not hard, but

loosely constructed. The spaces between individual grains may have been filled with ice.

From findings by future spacecraft and with continued, intensive observations from Earth, scientists hope to gain a better understanding of what comets are.

A typical comet away from the sun consists of a small nucleus of frozen gases, dust, and ice. As it approaches the sun, sunlight and the solar wind cause its outer layers to thaw, forming a cloud like halo (coma) around the nucleus and one or more tails of gas and dust. As the comet swings around the sun, the tails reach their greatest length. As the comet moves away from the sun, the coma and tails begin to dissipate. The tails always point away from the sun.

OTHER SUNS, OTHER REALMS

Beyond our solar system are immense numbers of stars, galaxies, and other objects that, along with vast stretches of empty space, make up the universe as we know it. This section of the book examines many of these objects, including the different types of stars and galaxies, nebulae, supernovae, pulsars, black holes, and quasars. Theories on the origin of the physical universe are also given, with particular emphasis on the big bang theory.

The Trifid nebula is a large ball of gas that is illuminated by stars shining within it. The Trifid is part of a large interstellar cloud located in our own Milky Way galaxy.

Galaxy M104, otherwise known as the Sombrero galaxy, displays a brightly glowing central bulge and a dark plane of interstellar dust and gas across the galaxy's center. It is about 40 million light-years from Earth.

This color-enhanced optical photograph of Galaxy NGC 1097 shows spiral arms made up of millions of stars radiating out from the galaxy's center.

CONSTELLATIONS

Have you ever spent an evening watching the stars? To look at these tiny pinpoints of light, it is nearly impossible to imagine that they are mighty suns. The gap between appearance and reality is too great.

Recall how the ancients saw the universe: a dome sky over the flat Earth. Since this is how the sky actually does appear, astronomers still find it useful to imagine a sky dome arching over Earth—at least when mapping the stars or aiming a telescope.

The sky dome visible at any one time from any one location is only half of all space. The other half is below the horizon. So, astronomers think not in

This seventeenth-century Czech drawing is a fanciful rendition of the constellations of the zodiac and some of the other major star groups. The heavier, wavy line in the center is the ecliptic, the apparent annual path the sun makes through the zodiac, as seen from Earth.

terms of a dome or hemisphere, but of a complete celestial sphere encircling Earth. The stars seem to be attached to its inside surface; we're at its center.

We know the celestial sphere is imaginary. It is only the apparent sky, not the real universe of endless space. But since this is the face the universe presents to our view, let's review some aspects of the sky as it appears from Earth.

PATTERNS IN THE SKY

From earliest times, people looking at the sky saw the stars in patterns—a triangle here, a zig-zag line there, a more complex group somewhere else. The same star patterns appeared night after night, year after year. The ancient shepherds and nomads who

This map shows the sky as it appears from the North Pole, with Polaris, the North Star, directly overhead. Elsewhere in the Northern Hemisphere, Polaris appears lower in the sky. To use the map, face south and turn the map so that the current month appears at the bottom. The stars in the bottom two-thirds of the map will be visible at some time of the night.

spent their lives under the open sky must have become intimately familiar with them.

These people saw the star patterns in terms of things they knew: animals, mythical characters, and various objects. In this way, the constellations were invented. The word *constellation* simply means "star group." Many familiar constellations, such as Taurus the Bull and Leo

the Lion, originated in Babylonia around 3000 B.C. or even earlier. They are among the oldest examples of ancient culture that have lasted into modern times.

To fill the holes between the ancient constellations, astronomers of more recent centuries invented some new ones. Still more were invented when European sailors first explored the Southern Hemisphere and saw a part of the sky never visible from northern lands. Today, the entire celestial sphere is divided

CETUS
Mira
SCULPTOR
Fomalhaut
PISCIS
AUSTRINUS
AQUARIUS
ERIDANUS
PHOENIX
GRUS
CAPRICORNUS
FORNAX
AQUILA
MICROSCOPIUM
Achernar
TUCANA
HOROLOGIUM
INDUS
SAGITTARIUS
SCUTUM
CAELUM
PAVO
CORONA AUSTRALIS
Rigel
DORADO
HYDRUS
RETICULUM
TELESCOPIUM
LEPUS
ORION
MENSA
OCTANS
APUS
ARA
SERPENS CAUDA
COLUMBA
VOLANS
CHAMAELEON
CANIS MAIOR
PICTOR
TRIANGULUM
AUSTRALE
SCORPIUS
OPHIUCHUS
Canopus
Sirius
CARINA
MUSCA
CIRCINUS
Antares
Acrux
NORMA
MONOCEROS
VELA
LUPUS
CRUX
PUPPIS
LIBRA
SERPENS
CAPUT
CENTAURUS
PYXIS
ANTLIA
HYDRA
HYDRA
Alphard
VIRGO
CRATER
CORVUS
Spica
SEXTANS
LEO

SEPTEMBER
OCTOBER
AUGUST
NOVEMBER
JULY
DECEMBER
JUNE
JANUARY
MAY
FEBRUARY
APRIL
MARCH

This map shows the sky as it appears from the South Pole. The constellation Octans is almost directly overhead. From other areas in the Southern Hemisphere, Octans appears lower in the sky. To use the map in the Southern Hemisphere, you would face north and turn the map so that the current month appears at the bottom.

into 88 constellations. Each is a distinct piece of sky territory with boundaries officially set by the International Astronomical Union, an international association of astronomers that is the controlling body of world astronomy.

The 88 constellations fill the sky with an odd jumble of creatures, mechanical objects, and mythical persons. Among them are Cepheus and Cassiopeia, a king and queen of Ethiopia; Andromeda, their daughter; Cetus, a sea monster the gods sent to devour her; and Perseus, her rescuer. Hercules, the legendary Greek hero, has a place in the sky. There is a ship, a sailor's sextant, a pair of scales, a clock, a telescope, and an air pump. Among the animals memorialized in the stars are two bears, a giraffe, a crab, two sea serpents, several dogs, a wolf, a crow, a rabbit, a lizard, and a fly.

Learning your way around the brighter constellations will give you a good practical grasp of the sky. But don't expect to see actual likenesses of lions and air pumps. Whatever was going on in the ancients' minds when they named the star patterns we'll never know. Perhaps they connected the stars to form stick figures suggesting the things named. The inventors of more modern constellations, including the machines, made no claim at all of trying to match names to shapes.

Once you know some of the star patterns, you'll be able to point out bright stars and planets by name. This is the first step to becoming an amateur astronomer. After all, you can't use a telescope until you know where to point it, and the constellations make up the map of the heavens.

108

STAR NAMES

The most prominent stars have names of their own. The brightest in the sky is Sirius in the constellation Canis Major, the Large Dog. Among the brightest stars visible from our north temperate latitudes are Arcturus in Boötes the Herdsman, Vega in Lyra the Harp, Capella in Auriga the Charioteer, and Rigel in Orion.

About 3,000 stars are visible to the naked eye on a clear, dark night. Few people could remember 3,000 separate names for them. Instead, astronomers use a system that was invented in 1603 by Johann Bayer, a German lawyer who mapped the sky in

his spare time. Bayer labeled the stars in each constellation with Greek letters, roughly in order of brightness. Thus, Sirius is Alpha of Canis Major. The phrase is given in Latin: Alpha Canis Majoris. Vega is named Alpha Lyrae, and Capella is Alpha Aurigae.

Other astronomers gave letters to the fainter stars Bayer's system missed. Still others numbered the stars in each constellation. These systems are quite convenient because they tell in what sky territory a star is located. Beta Cygni and 61 Cygni, for instance, are both in the constellation of Cygnus, the Swan.

This illustration shows the 12 signs of the zodiac. Note that the star patterns bear no real resemblance to the figures they portray. The zodiacal signs are used today primarily to identify different parts of the night sky.

It should be stressed that the constellation patterns are only apparent, not real. When you see a few stars forming an apparent pattern in the sky, they probably are not at all like that pattern in three-dimensional space. One star can be many times farther away than another that seems right next to it; they're merely lined up in our line of sight. The four stars forming the Great Square of Pegasus, for example, are at distances of 70, 100, 180, and 500 light-years, so they actually have nothing to do with each other. A light-year is the distance that light travels in one year. Since light travels at the speed of 186,282 miles per second, one light-year is approximately 6 trillion miles.

STAR BRIGHTNESSES

The ancient Greek astronomers called the brightest stars first magnitude, meaning "largest."

Slightly fainter ones they called second magnitude, and so on down to the faintest that can be seen, which they called sixth magnitude.

In modern times, this scale has been extended both to fainter and brighter objects. When the telescope was invented, it showed stars too dim to see with the naked eye; these were named seventh magnitude, eighth magnitude, and so on. Eventually, the system was put on an exact mathematical basis, so star brightnesses could be measured accurately. Today, a pair of binoculars will show stars of eighth or ninth magnitude, an average amateur telescope reveals stars of twelfth magnitude, and the largest telescopes in the world are able to detect stars down to about twenty-fifth magnitude.

At the same time, it was realized that some first-magnitude stars are much brighter than others. So the scale was extended upward to zero magnitude, for stars like Vega and Capella, and into negative numbers. The planet Venus gets as bright as magnitude -4.7, the full moon is magnitude -12, and the sun is magnitude -27. This system of magnitudes is encountered in every branch of astronomy.

MOTIONS OF THE SKY

As the hours of the night wear on, stars set in the west and new ones rise in the east. We know it is Earth that is turning, not the stars. But it looks as if the celestial sphere rotates around us while we stand still.

If we are viewing the heavens from Earth's Northern Hemisphere, the entire sky appears to pivot on what is called the north celestial pole. This is the point in the sky directly above the Earth's North Pole. Very near this point is a famous star, Polaris, otherwise known as the North Star. It's not very bright (second magnitude), but it isn't hard to find, because the two stars at the end of the Big Dipper's bowl point almost directly at it.

Stars in the sky all appear to be the same distance from us, but they are not. This diagram shows the Big Dipper as we see it (right) and the actual distances of the stars (center) from Earth.

The objects of our solar system—the sun, moon, and planets—appear to move among the stars. The sun appears to circle the celestial sphere once a year. This appearance, of course, is caused by Earth orbiting around the sun. As a result, we see different constellations in the night sky—that is, in directions away from the sun—at different times of the year. The Great Square of Pegasus is in the evening sky of autumn; Sirius is a winter star; Vega lights the evenings of spring and summer.

The sun's apparent path across the sky is called the ecliptic. The moon and planets also follow the ecliptic fairly closely. This well-traveled path crosses 12 major constellations known as the zodiac. These are the constellations in which the sun, moon, and planets are almost always found.

Thousands of years ago, when the planets were associated with gods or spirits or looked on as some sort of occult objects, they were assumed to influence human affairs. The study of astrology was the attempt to chart this influence, which was supposed to depend on the positions of the sun, moon, and planets in relation to the constellations of the zodiac.

Today, we know the planets and stars are physical objects and are much too far away to have any effect on human affairs. In case there was any doubt, careful studies have searched thoroughly for the slightest match-up between people's astrological charts and their lives or personalities. There turns out to be no connection at all.

On the other hand, the truth about the stars is far stranger and more amazing than anything the medieval astrologers could have dreamed up. It is to these distant suns that we now turn.

111

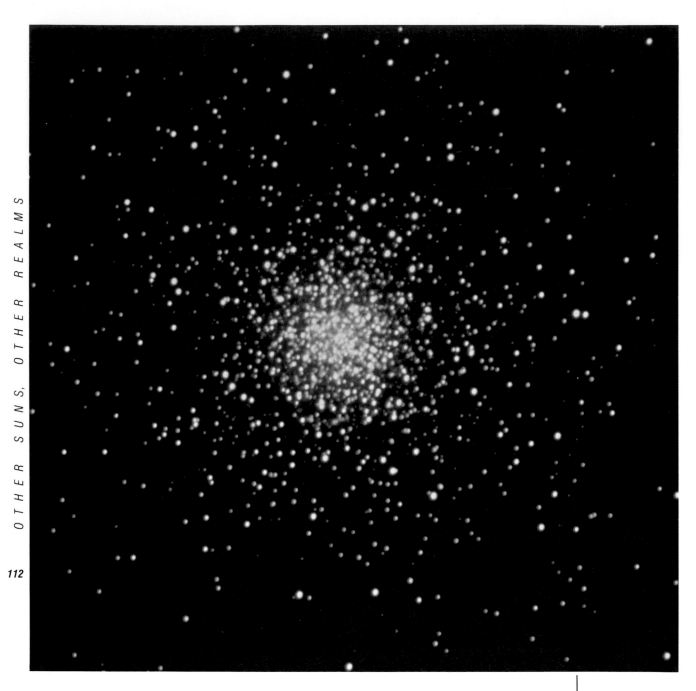

STARS

A star is a gigantic ball of hot gas, so hot it glows. Our sun is a very average example, as stars go. Some are much larger than the sun, some much smaller; some are many times brighter, some far dimmer. The sun falls about midway between the extremes; in fact, it is a little on the small and dim side.

Even so, the sun is a stupendous object 865,000 miles (1,384,000 kilometers) in diameter—wider than over 100 Earths. Its surface temperature is about

Stars are the most common objects in the universe—more than 200 billion billion. M3, pictured here, is a globular cluster containing millions of stars, most of which are concentrated in the center of the cluster.

10,000° F. (5,500° C), hotter than almost any flame that can be created on Earth. Using carefully protected and filtered telescopes, astronomers find that the sun's surface is an extremely violent, boiling sea of hot gases marked by vast upheavals, stormlike activities, and explosions many times larger than Earth itself.

Yet compared to most of the stars visible to the naked eye, the sun is small. Sirius is quite a bit hotter and larger and shines with 30 times more light. Vega is 50 times brighter than the sun; Rigel puts forth 15,500 times more light.

Stars are made up mostly of hydrogen and helium. This is the key to where they get their energy. Deep inside a star, the temperature may be tens of millions of degrees; at the sun's core, the temperature is over 27,000,000° F. (15,000,000° C). This is hot enough to set off a nuclear reaction that combines hydrogen nuclei to form helium. This is the reaction that powers a hydrogen bomb. A star is like a giant, continuous H-bomb that uses its nuclear fuel steadily rather than exploding all at once.

In the 1800's, before nuclear energy was discovered, the source of the sun's power was a great puzzle. No one had any idea what could keep the sun burning for so long. If the sun were made of coal, astronomers calculated that it could shine at its present brightness for only a few thousand years before burning up completely. If it were slowly shrinking, it could gain heat from gravitational energy, but only enough for 100 million years. Geological evidence proved that Earth had been warm for much longer than this. The mystery of what powers the sun was a major spur leading to the discovery of nuclear energy. Nuclear reactions, as we shall see, are the key to understanding the lives, and eventual deaths, of all stars.

HOW HOT, HOW BIG, HOW BRIGHT?

One thing can usually be known about a star just by looking at it: its temperature. Some stars are merely red-hot, such as Betelgeuse and Antares. They have a distinctly reddish tint even at a casual glance. Other stars are orange-hot. Some, like Capella, are yellow-hot. The sun is yellow-white hot, Polaris white hot. Others such as Vega and Rigel are even blue-white-hot. This is the same sequence of colors that

Stellar parallax can be used to determine the distance to a nearby star. A nearby star's position against a background of distant stars seems to shift as the star is viewed from opposite ends of Earth's orbit. One-half of the angle formed by the "lines of vision" is known as the stellar (or trigonometrical) parallax. The radius of Earth's orbit is one Astronomical Unit (AU), 93 million miles (149 million kilometers). Knowing the parallax and the radius of Earth's orbit, trigonometry is used to calculate the distance to the star.

113

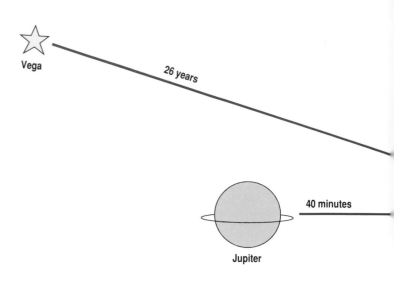

What is a Light-Year?

A light-year is the distance light travels in a year at a speed of 186,282 miles (298,051 kilometers) per second. This distance is 5.88 trillion miles (9.41 trillion kilometers). Light reflected from the moon takes about 1.25 seconds to reach Earth. The sun's rays travel for about 8.33 minutes before they reach us. Light reflected from Jupiter takes 40 minutes to reach Earth. The light emitted from Vega takes 26 light-years to travel the trillions of miles separating this nearby star from our solar system. The light we see from the Andromeda galaxy, the nearest major galaxy to our own, is already 2.2 million years old when it reaches us.

Andromeda Galaxy

objects on Earth—from an electric stove coil to a light-bulb filament—go through when heated enough.

But most facts about a star cannot be known just by looking. Among these are its distance and true brightness. Sirius and Rigel appear not far apart in the winter sky. How can Sirius look brighter if it is only 23 times as luminous as the sun while Rigel is 15,500 times as luminous? The answer is that Sirius is only 8.8 light-years away, a very near neighbor as stars go, while Rigel is about 900 light-years distant. The light we see from Sirius left it just 8.8 years ago. The light that strikes our eyes today from Rigel has been traveling through space for so long that it was only a little more than halfway here when Columbus first landed in the Americas.

The most luminous stars blaze several hundred thousand times the sun's light. At the other extreme, the dimmest stars emit

Moon 1.25 seconds

Earth

8.33 minutes

Sun

twentieth the mass of the sun, the largest only 100 times the sun's material.

STAR CLASSIFICATION

When all this variety began to be discovered among stars, astronomers developed a way to categorize them and find the order beneath the confusion. They placed the stars on a chart called the Hertzsprung-Russell diagram, which is named after the two astronomers who invented it. Stars are arranged by temperature from left to right, and by true brightness from top to bottom. The chart has been a basic tool for categorizing and understanding stars since its invention in the early 1900's.

Those stars that lie at the top of the diagram—the extremely luminous stars—are called supergiants; hot blue ones are toward the left, cooler red ones toward the right. Below these are ordinary giants. Another variety of stars falls on a curving band from upper left to lower right. This is called the main sequence. These are normal, hydrogen-burning stars like our sun—which can be found near the middle of the band.

less than one one-hundred thousandth the light of the sun. If such a feeble star were to replace our sun, we would receive little more light from it than we now get reflected off a full moon.

The size of a star is another quantity impossible to know just by looking. Stars are so far away that they appear as pinpoints in any telescope, no matter how powerful. But they have almost as extreme a range of sizes as brightnesses. The biggest may be 1 billion miles (1.6 billion kilometers) or more across. It would take light fully an hour and a half just to cross the face of such a monstrous object; our sun, by comparison, is only 4.6 light-seconds across.

Other stars are as small as a few thousand miles in diameter,

and in the most extreme cases, less than 10 miles (16 kilometers) in diameter. Such an object might fit within the borders of your hometown. These are the neutron stars, extraordinary objects made of extremely dense nuclear material. They have densities, gravities, hardnesses, and magnetic field strengths beyond imagining.

Clearly, the word *star* covers an enormously broad range of different objects. If you put the brightest and faintest ones next to each other, the difference would be greater than that between a high-power searchlight and a tiny spark of glowing ash. The difference in size between the smallest and largest would be the difference between a speck of dust and a gas balloon 1 mile (1.6 kilometers) across.

However, stars are much more alike in one very important respect: the actual amount of material they contain. The least massive ones have about one-

115

Giant

Main sequence star

White dwarf

Neutron star

Supergiant

This illustration
shows the great dif-
ferences in the sizes
of stars. Astronomers
divide stars into five
groups by size, which
in almost all of these
groups still varies
greatly. Most stars
are main sequence
stars of medium size,
like the sun. Stars
called giants have a
diameter from 10 to
100 times that of the
sun. Supergiants, the
largest stars, have a
diameter 100 to 1,000
times that of the sun.
A few white dwarfs
are smaller than
Earth. Neutron stars,
the smallest stars, are
only about 11 miles in
diameter.

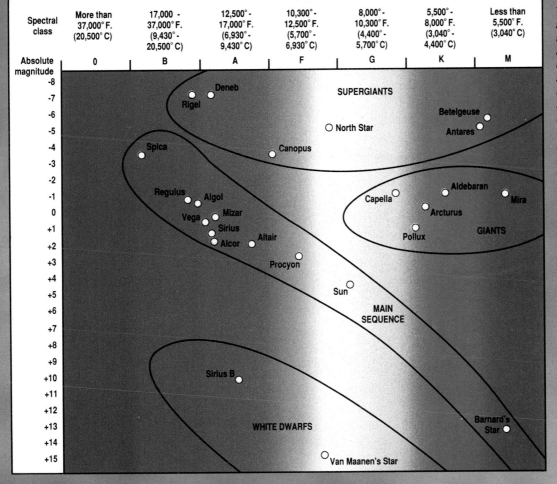

Spectral class	More than 37,000° F. (20,500° C)	17,000 - 37,000° F. (9,430° - 20,500° C)	12,500° - 17,000° F. (6,930° - 9,430° C)	10,300° - 12,500° F. (5,700° - 6,930° C)	8,000° - 10,300° F. (4,400° - 5,700° C)	5,500° - 8,000° F. (3,040° - 4,400° C)	Less than 5,500° F. (3,040° C)
	O	B	A	F	G	K	M

Absolute magnitude

-8
-7
-6
-5
-4
-3
-2
-1
0
+1
+2
+3
+4
+5
+6
+7
+8
+9
+10
+11
+12
+13
+14
+15

Deneb
Rigel
SUPERGIANTS
Betelgeuse
North Star
Antares
Spica
Canopus
Aldebaran
Regulus
Capella
Mira
Algol
Arcturus
Vega
Mizar
Sirius
Pollux
GIANTS
Alcor
Altair
Procyon
Sun
MAIN SEQUENCE
Sirius B
Barnard's Star
WHITE DWARFS
Van Maanen's Star

The Hertzsprung-Russell diagram helps astronomers classify and study stars. The color bands illustrate spectral classes identified by the letters and temperatures across the top of the diagram. A star is represented on the diagram by a dot located horizontally according to the star's spectral class and vertically according to its absolute magnitude. For example, the sun belongs to spectral class G and has an absolute magnitude of +5. This combination puts the sun on the main sequence.

Main-sequence stars are called dwarfs to distinguish them from giants; thus the sun is a yellow dwarf. Among the dimmest stars of all are the red dwarfs, like Barnard's Star, at the bottom of the main sequence. White dwarfs are a peculiar class off by themselves. Neutron stars are beyond the diagram's lower right edge. We will return to all of these types as we follow the evolution of a typical star from its birth through its youth, middle age, and eventual death.

Notice the capital letters across the top of the diagram. These are spectral classes, which

A planetarium theater has special facilities for presenting programs about the stars and the solar system. The large projector in the middle of the theater creates an image of the sky on the domed ceiling.

is the most widely used way of sorting stars into distinctive groups. Among other things, a star's spectral type tells its temperature very accurately.

A star's light can be broken up into its different colors, or wavelengths, by sending it through a prism—the same way a prism will break up a ray of sunlight into rainbow colors. The array of colors is called a spectrum. A star's spectrum is marked by many fine lines at different wavelengths. These are called spectral lines, and they are a star's individual fingerprint. Each chemical element or compound causes its own set of spectral lines at different temperatures. So, by analyzing the lines, astronomers can tell a star's temperature and chemical composition.

Spectral types form a smooth sequence from the hottest to coolest stars. The order of this spectral sequence, as can be seen on the diagram, is O B A F G K M, with type O stars being the hottest blue-white ones and type M those that are only red-hot. Our sun is type G.

DOUBLES AND MULTIPLES

Some stars that look single to the naked eye are seen in a telescope actually to be close pairs. The first of these double stars to be discovered was Mizar, the middle star in the handle of the Big Dipper. Other prominent doubles are Albireo (Beta Cygni), Castor (Alpha Geminorum), and Epsilon Lyrae. These and hundreds more are lovely sights in a small telescope.

The two stars of a double are truly close together in space, bound together by their gravity. They orbit each other the same way planets orbit the sun.

Doubles come in almost every possible combination of star types. And they have all possible distances apart. Some pairs are so close that the stars almost touch; these orbit each other very rapidly, as quickly as once an hour. Others are farther apart and orbit more slowly. Some pairs, separated by almost a light-year, take millions of years to complete one orbit around each other.

The closest doubles cannot be separated with the best telescopes. Astronomers instead find them by indirect techniques. When all doubles are tallied, they actually turn out to be slightly more common than single stars.

In addition, some stars are triple, quadruple, quintuple, and up. It is fascinating to figure out what the days would be like on a planet in a multiple star system. Such planets probably do exist. There might be worlds where a sun like ours is rising in the east while a red-giant sun blazes down from high overhead and a tiny, brilliant blue sun is setting in the west—making it dawn, noon, and evening all at once.

VARIABLE STARS

The sun, luckily for us, keeps putting out the same steady amount of light and heat day after day, year after year. But certain other stars vary in brightness, often dramatically. They are known as variable stars.

One type of variable star isn't truly variable at all. Sometimes a close double is oriented so that every time the pair circle each other, one star eclipses, or blocks, our view of the other. So we see the total light of the system diminish and then return to normal once per orbit. These are called eclipsing binary stars. The most famous example, and the first discovered, is Algol (Beta Persei). It loses two-thirds of its brightness every 2 days and 21 hours. This eclipsing of its light lasts about five hours.

Other variable stars are single stars that really do change their light output. They come in almost countless varieties. One class is the pulsating variable stars. An example of this type is the red giant Mira in the constellation Cetus; its changes in brightness can be followed with the naked eye. Pulsating variables change radically in brightness within a period of a few hours to many years. Cepheid variables, another type of pulsating variable, pulsate with shorter periods usually lasting about one week.

Another class is the exploding variables. These are stars that burst from time to time. Some undergo a relatively small outburst—increasing just a few magnitudes in brightness—every few days or weeks. Others, the recurring novae, explode more vigorously every few decades. The true novae are those that have only been seen to explode once, and with still greater violence. Even they, however, are believed to survive the event to explode again every few thousand years.

Only the outer layer of a star is involved in a nova explosion; the rest of the star remains intact. A supernova, however, destroys a star entirely. This is by far the most spectacular stellar event. A supernova is seen in our galaxy only rarely—the last one was seen in 1604—but it can become the brightest star in the sky for several weeks and can even sometimes be seen in broad daylight.

Many other kinds of variables enliven the sky. Some stars shine at their normal brightness for months or years at a time and then suddenly fade without warning. And there are stars called irregular variables that follow no clear pattern at all.

Amateur astronomers have contributed a great deal to this branch of astronomy by monitoring the variations of hundreds of stars for decades. Professional astronomers, in turn, have found the study of variables to be especially valuable for probing the inner workings of all stars and for helping to figure out their life histories from birth to death.

Friedrich Wilhelm Bessel (1784–1846), a German astronomer and mathematician, was the first person to measure the distance to a star other than the sun.

121

NEBULAE AND THE BIRTH OF STARS

A nebula is a cloud of dust particles and gases in space. The emission nebula (lower left) *is brightly lit up by stars from within it. The Horse-head nebula (right) is so filled with dust and gas, that any starlight from behind it is blotted out.*

So-called empty space is not to-tally empty. Even between the stars there is an extremely thin trace of gas, mostly hydrogen. It averages about one atom per cu-bic centimeter. This is still far closer to a perfect vacuum than the best vacuum that can be made on Earth.

Mixed in with the thin gas are traces of dust particles. Each mi-croscopic particle is approxi-mately 300 feet (900 meters) from the next. But the volume of space is so huge that these traces

orescent lamp. Or the dust particles can reflect starlight directly,
forming a reflection nebula.

A dark nebula is another type.
It doesn't glow at all and can be
seen silhouetted against a starry
background. Some dark nebulae
are visible to the naked eye. If
you have a very dark, rural sky,
you can see the band of the
Milky Way crossing overhead in
the summer; it appears spotted
with patchy dark nebulae blot-
ting out the light of stars behind
them.

In some nebulae, many bright
stars are mixed in with the
clouds. They are there by no coincidence. Nebulae are where all
stars are born.

STAR BIRTH

If a cloud of interstellar matter
is dense enough, it starts to contract under the force of its own
gravity. Every bit of matter in it
attracts every other bit, with the
result that all parts of the cloud
start falling together. The
smaller the cloud gets, the faster
it shrinks. Material falling in
from different sides collides in
the middle and remains there,
and more material rains down

of interstellar matter add up to
an important amount.

In some places, the interstellar
gas and dust is a bit thicker than
in others. If a relatively thick
cloud happens to lie near a star,
the cloud is lit up, forming a
bright nebula. A well-known example is in the constellation Orion. A pair of binoculars is all
that is needed to see the Great
Nebula of Orion. It looks like a
hazy, multi-colored mist surrounding the middle stars in Orion's sword.

A nebula (Latin for "cloud")
can shine in two ways. The gas
can fluoresce, or glow, under the
influence of a star's ultraviolet
light, much like the gas in a flu-

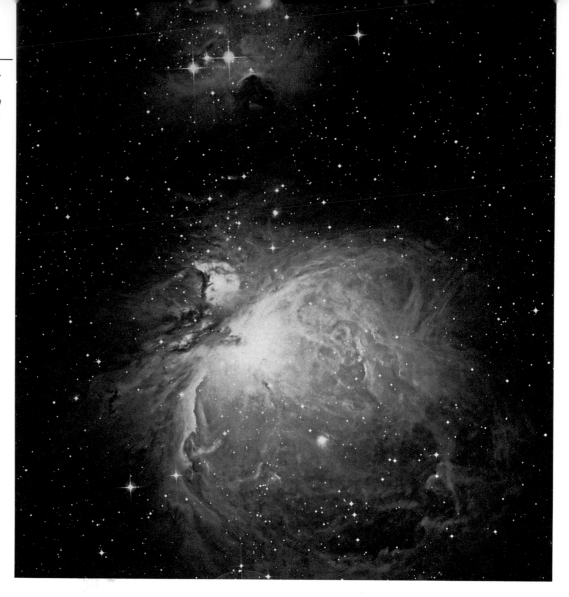

Sixteen hundred light-years from Earth, stars are continuing to form in the Great Nebula of Orion. The reddish streaks are huge quantities of energized hydrogen gas.

These two photographs show what may be new stars forming in a dust-and-gas cloud. The photograph on the left, taken in 1947, shows three stars in the cloud. The photograph on the right, taken in 1954, shows two outgrowths on two of the stars. These outgrowths may be new stars forming from the "parent" stars.

onto it. This mass at the center of the cloud heats up under the impact of all the infalling material. At this point, the object is called a protostar.

As the protostar becomes denser and hotter, pressure builds up at its center and slows its shrinking. Eventually, the heat and pressure in the center become great enough to ignite the nuclear reaction that converts hydrogen to helium. This nuclear activity provides abundant heat—enough to halt the star from shrinking any further. It shines brilliantly, and any of the surrounding cloud that remains in the vicinity is dispersed.

The star has now arrived on the main sequence of the Hertzsprung-Russell diagram. Here it will remain for much of its life, slowly using up its hydrogen fuel.

Any planets that orbit a star are formed at the same time. If the original cloud had any internal motions or rotation—which is very likely—then some of the material will form a thick disk of gas and dust orbiting the newborn star. Within this disk, smaller masses of gas and dust are expected to collapse and become planets. This is presumably how our own solar system formed. Today, we see such disks surrounding a number of stars that are in the process of being born. We could be witnessing future solar systems in the making.

STAR CLUSTERS

Stars are generally born in great bunches rather than singly. A cloud that starts collapsing may contain enough matter for many thousands of stars. Indeed, a nebula often contains many groups of stars, called star clusters.

As time goes on, the nebula is consumed to form more stars or is blown away. Left behind is one or more clusters. Dozens of such clusters are visible in binoculars or a small telescope. The most famous is the Pleiades in the constellation Taurus. It is easily visible to the naked eye in the winter sky as a little glittering cloud. Long-exposure photographs of the Pleiades reveal the last wisps of the dusty nebula from which its stars were born.

After many millions of years, a cluster is likely to break up entirely, with each star going its own separate way. That is why many stars, including the sun, eventually travel alone.

Star Formation

A star begins forming from a collapsing cloud of gas and dust (left). As the cloud continues to collapse, the central area begins to heat up, forming a protostar (center). The central area eventually becomes hot enough to ignite a continuous nuclear reaction. The collapsing ceases, and the result is a main-sequence star.

125

MAIN-SEQUENCE STARS

Once a star is born, it stays at the same brightness and temperature for much of its life. If it were to shrink any further, the pressure and temperature at its core would rise, causing the nuclear reaction to occur at a faster rate and create more energy,

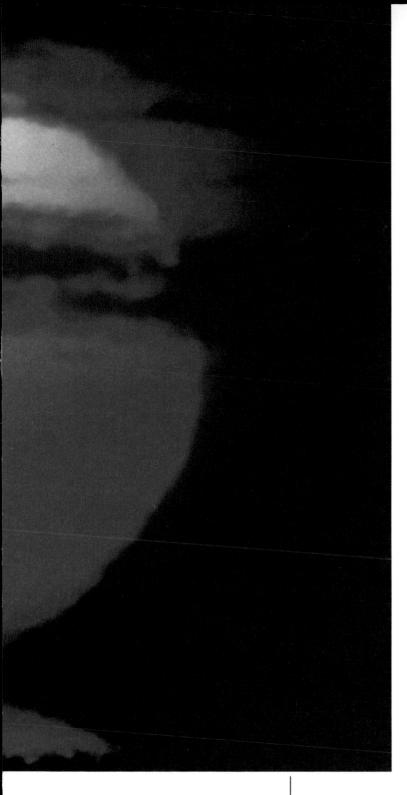

Our sun is a main-sequence star. It releases energy at a steady rate and will remain about the same size for most of its life.

which would expand the star again. If something caused it to swell, it would cool and the reaction would slow, releasing less energy and allowing the star to contract again under the squeeze of its gravity. So it does not change either way. Any system in such a situation is said to be in equilibrium. The sun is a good example.

Recall the Hertzsprung-Russell diagram. The band of the main sequence represents stars that haven't changed much since birth. Note the enormous range in brightness. Some are many times brighter than the sun, and some are many times fainter. What causes some stars to burn so brightly and others to glow so dimly?

The answer is simply their mass. A star that is formed with a lot of material—30 times the sun's mass, let's say—has intense gravity pulling it together, so the pressure at its core is high. The nuclear reaction that converts hydrogen to helium then proceeds very fast. A tremendous amount of energy is released. The result is a brilliant, blue-white star at the top of the main sequence. Examples are the stars of Orion's Belt.

A star with just a couple of times the sun's mass will be farther up the main sequence from the sun. Sirius is an example. Astronomers call the mass of the sun one solar mass. A star with only one-twelfth of a solar mass burns its hydrogen so slowly that it is a feeble red dwarf at the bottom of the main sequence. Barnard's Star is an example of a red dwarf.

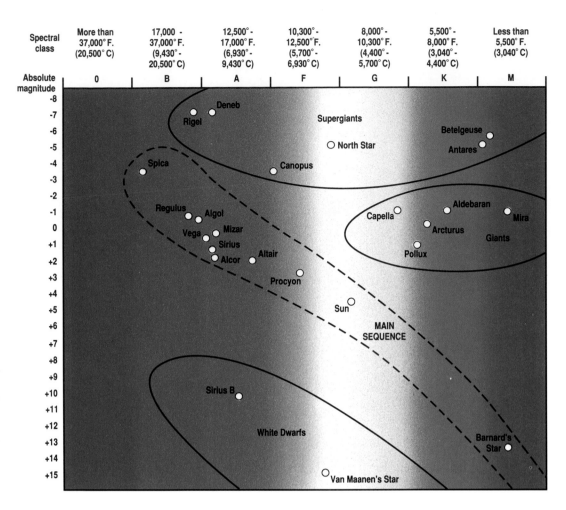

Spectral class	More than 37,000° F. (20,500° C)	17,000 - 37,000° F. (9,430° - 20,500° C)	12,500° - 17,000° F. (6,930° - 9,430° C)	10,300° - 12,500° F. (5,700° - 6,930° C)	8,000° - 10,300° F. (4,400° - 5,700° C)	5,500° - 8,000° F. (3,040° - 4,400° C)	Less than 5,500° F. (3,040° C)
	O	B	A	F	G	K	M

Main-sequence stars come in a wide variety of brightness and temperatures. Such stars as Spica, Regulus, and Algol are very massive objects that are extremely hot and bright. Other main-sequence stars, such as Barnard's Star, are dim, relatively cool stars.

The faster a star burns, the sooner its fuel will be used up. The brightest stars are using up their fuel at a very fast pace. Even though they have more fuel to use, they will last only a few million years, which is a very short time for the life of a star.

The sun, using its hydrogen more prudently, has a lifetime on the main sequence of about 9 or 10 billion years. Red dwarfs will outlast all other types of stars in the universe, shining on in their modest way for hundreds of billions of years. In the inconceivably remote future, there may be a time when no stars remain but red dwarfs.

4.6 billion years old. That is how long it has been since the sun and planets condensed out of a collapsing cloud of interstellar gas and dust. We know approximately how much hydrogen fuel the sun contains, and we know about how fast it is being used up. So we can estimate how much longer the sun will shine. The answer is reassuring: the sun will light and warm Earth steadily for another 5 billion years.

After that time, the sun will swell to become a red giant star and Earth will be doomed. But this ultimate fate of Earth is of no immediate concern to the human race. It is too far away.

THE LIFE OF THE SUN AND EARTH

Where are we in the life of our own star? The sun, Earth, and the rest of the solar system are

128

To grasp the time involved in the lives of the sun and Earth, let's consider a scale model. We can represent the 4.6-billion-year age of the solar system by the height of the World Trade Center in New York City; it is a skyscraper 110 stories—1,350 feet (405 meters)—tall. On this scale, a million years is just 3.5 inches (8.75 centimeters). Earth and the sun formed at ground level. Most early multicellular forms of life—mud worms and the like—didn't evolve until about 600 million years ago, or around the 95th floor. About 420 million years ago—the 100th floor—the first primitive plants and animals came out of the sea onto land.

The dinosaurs lived for a period of time represented by the 104th to the 108th floors. The earliest humans appeared about 2 million years ago, only 7 inches from the ceiling of the 110th floor. All recorded history, all civilization, lies in the last 5,000 years—the layer of paint one-fiftieth of an inch thick on the ceiling of the 110th floor.

Yet, the history that lies ahead for Earth and the sun amounts to a whole additional 110-story building placed on top of the first. Earth has a much longer future ahead of it than the time since the first grubs lived in the mud of the ocean. We may think we are the crown of creation, but the history of life on Earth is clearly just beginning. The death of the sun, so far into the inconceivable future, cannot possibly concern us.

Yet even today, we see in the sky many stars much older than the sun. We can point out stars similar to the sun that are 9 or 10 billion years old and coming to the end of their lives on the main sequence. Their hydrogen is nearly used up, and already they are beginning to swell into the bloated and monstrous forms that characterize the later parts of a star's life. To this stage we now turn.

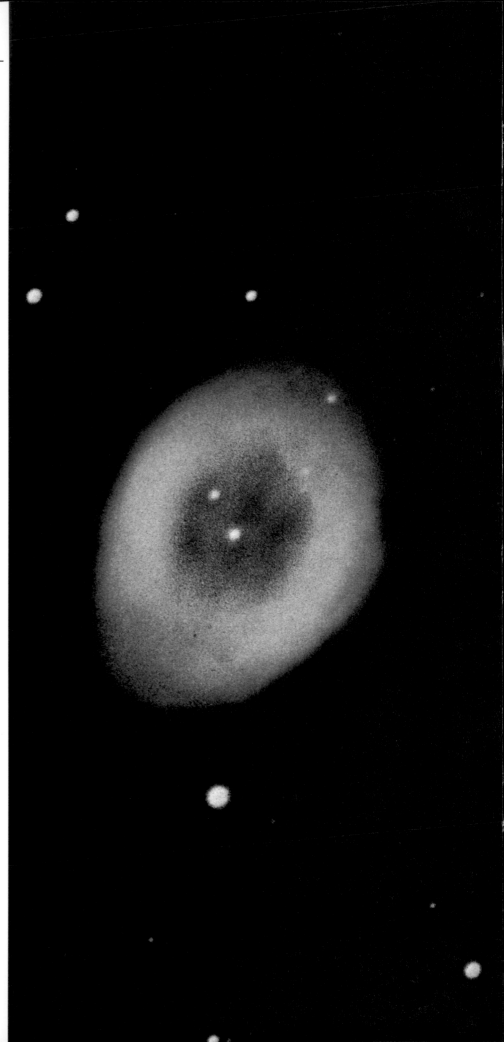

The Ring nebula, pictured here, resulted when the bright star in the middle of the nebula blew off its outer layers into space, forming a cloudlike halo of dust and gases. Such an occurrence is called a planetary nebula. It is fairly common toward the end of life for certain kinds of stars.

RED GIANTS, WHITE DWARFS

Nothing is forever. As ages roll on, the interior of a main-sequence star slowly begins to change. Its hydrogen fuel is used up, and helium piles up in its core. The zone where nuclear reactions take place moves from the center closer to the surface. The entire star begins to expand—slowly at first, then with increasing speed.

The star is becoming a red giant. It eventually swells to dozens or even hundreds of times its original size. Its surface cools to the point of being only

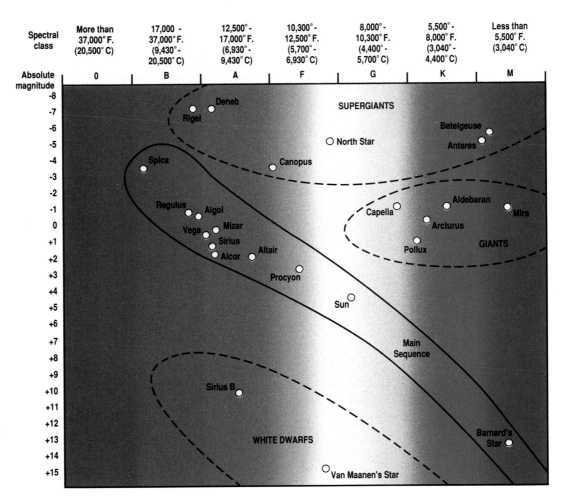

Red giants, super-giants, and white dwarfs are stars nearing the ends of their life cycles. The giants and supergiants are extremely large, bright objects with a wide range in temperature. White dwarfs are the small, dim, cooling remains of dying stars.

red-hot, but it has become so large that its total output of light and heat is much greater than before. Any planets nearby will be roasted and possibly melted, or they may be actually engulfed in the expanding giant.

Once the sun starts swelling, some 5 billion years from now, it will take another several hundred million years to grow into a full-blown red giant. At that time, it will be about 70 to 100 times larger than now—a gigantic fireball filling much of the sky. It will pour out 500 to 1,000 times more light than at present, heating our Earth to somewhere around 2,000° F. (1,100° C). The seas will have long since boiled away, and the atmosphere itself will be driven off into space. The world will be bare rock under a gigantic orange sun in a black sky.

Examples of stars that are already at this stage are Aldebaran in the constellation Taurus and Arcturus in Bootes.

Stars that are more massive than the sun burn brighter when on the main sequence, use up their hydrogen much faster, and expand more quickly. Red supergiants, such as Betelgeuse, are the result. These are the largest

This series of illustrations shows the sequence of events that lead to the death of a star like the sun (above).

As the star uses up its hydrogen supply in the core, the zone where nuclear reactions occur moves outward, and the star begins expanding.

The star's core, now made of helium, continues to shrink and becomes very dense. The outer portion of the star continues to expand, and the star becomes a full-blown red giant.

stars of all. Betelgeuse is roughly 400 million miles (640 million kilometers) across; if it were put in the place of the sun, it would fill the solar system out beyond the orbit of Mars.

LAST GASPS

A star cannot remain a red giant for very long, usually only about a tenth of the time it spent on the main sequence; it is running out of fuel. The helium core shrinks and becomes so dense and hot that another nuclear reaction starts: the fusing of helium to become carbon. This reaction provides some more energy and helps keep the star alive for a while longer. But it is shrinking and losing brilliance.

The star becomes hotter as it shrinks, moving to the left on the Hertzsprung-Russell diagram. At this stage, it is likely

to become a pulsating variable. The late stages of a star's life can be quite complex, depending on its mass. We will continue to follow what happens to one like the sun.

As time goes on, the star becomes still more unstable. Finally, a large part of its outer portions is gently blown off into space. This gas becomes a great bubble-shaped nebula around the remaining bare stellar core. This tiny core is extremely hot, so it emits great amounts of ultraviolet light, which causes the bubble to glow.

Many nebulae of this kind are visible in a telescope. They can be recognized by their roundness or symmetry and the fact that each is centered around a very

132

Eventually, a large part of the star's outer portion is blown gently off into space, leaving behind a cooling, shrinking, and bare stellar core.

As the stellar core slowly cools, it becomes a white dwarf, which is an object weighing as much as the sun yet only about as large as Earth.

When the star has completely spent its energy supply, it becomes a black dwarf, which is a cold, lightless stellar corpse.

hot blue star. Early observers named them planetary nebulae, because their roundness gave them a dim, ghostly resemblance to the way a planet looks in a telescope.

A planetary nebula lasts only a very short time astronomically—a few tens of thousands of years. Within this time, it disperses into space, rejoining the interstellar gas and dust out of which the star condensed so long ago.

The tiny star remaining has no more sources of energy. It slowly cools down and loses its brightness, moving to the lower portion of the Hertzsprung-Russell diagram and entering the realm of the white dwarfs.

DEAD STARS

When white dwarfs were discovered, they were almost too strange to be believed. One of the first to be found orbits the

nearby star Sirius. Astronomers in the 1800's measured the positions of stars very accurately, and they found that Sirius was wobbling back and forth by a tiny amount every 50 years. This could only be happening if Sirius were a double star, orbiting with an unseen companion.

In 1862, this companion was seen for the first time. Telescope maker Alvan Clark first spotted it while he was testing a large telescope lens. The companion became known as Sirius B. Its true brightness was found to be very slight: several hundred times dimmer than our sun. Yet its gravitational effect on Sirius showed it had to have very nearly the sun's mass.

There the matter rested until 1915, when the spectrum of Sirius B was photographed for the first time. This strange star, it turned out, is quite a bit hotter than the sun. So each square foot of its surface must be giving off more light than a square foot of the sun's surface. This leads to the conclusion that Sirius B is remarkably small. In fact, it is only about 6,500 miles (10,400 kilometers) in diameter. It is a star smaller than Earth.

To pack the sun's mass into such a small volume, Sirius B must be made of extremely dense material, thousands of times denser than lead. Its average density works out to about 70 tons per cubic inch (4.2 met-

This artist's conception of the sun as seen from Earth's surface several billion years from now shows the sun expanded into a red giant. All water will boil away, and life will cease to exist.

134

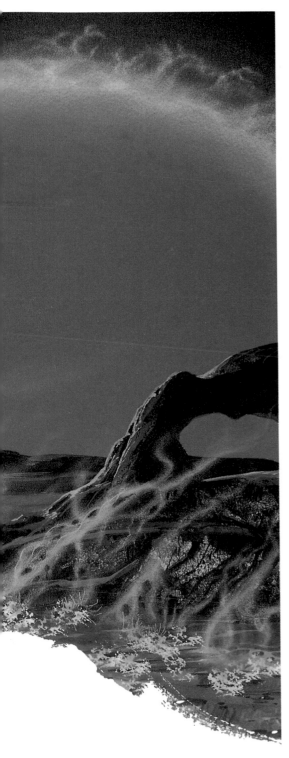

ric tons per cubic centimeter).
On Earth, a single teaspoonful of
its matter would weigh more
than a heavy truck.

The very idea of such material
at first seemed impossible. Yet it
had to be true. Other white
dwarf stars were soon found.
One of them, named 40 Eridani
B, is easy to see in a small amateur telescope.

Understanding white dwarf
material requires knowing how
matter is put together. In ordinary objects, atoms are packed
close together and cannot be
squeezed any more. This is why
ordinary solids and liquids are
incompressible. But an atom itself is mostly empty space.

A very lightweight shell of
electrons determines an atom's
size, but its tiny nucleus contains most of its mass. A scale
model of an atom would be an
empty gymnasium with a fly in
the middle—the gymnasium
being the electron shell and the
fly being the heavy nucleus.

Inside a white dwarf, material
is so compressed by gravity that
the atoms themselves are
crushed. In our scale model, the
gymnasium-sized electron shells
are broken up, and the nuclei—
the flies—lie much closer together. That is how so much
mass can fit in a small volume.

The strength of gravity on a
white dwarf is tremendous. The
gravity at the surface of Sirius B
is about 500,000 times stronger
than on Earth. If you weigh 150
pounds (68 kilograms) here, you
would weigh about 38,000 tons
(34,200 metric tons) on Sirius B
and would instantly be squashed
by your own weight into a thin
film on the surface. Since a cubic inch (16 cubic centimeters)
of Sirius B would weigh 70 tons
(63 metric tons) on Earth, it
must weigh 35 million tons
(31.5 million metric tons) where
it actually is. On top of all this,
many white dwarfs have magnetic fields thousands of times
stronger than the most powerful
magnets on Earth.

When the sun becomes a
white dwarf, it will shine with
about one-hundredth the brightness it has now. Earth, after having been roasted into a bare hulk
of rock during the sun's red
giant phase, will now be about
−300° F. (−184° C) and getting
colder. The dying sun will be a
dazzling white pinpoint in a
black sky.

For perhaps billions of years
more, the white dwarf sun will
slowly cool and dim, eventually
becoming a cold, lightless black
dwarf. This is the ultimate
corpse of a star like the sun, the
way it will remain forever after.
Earth will be in perpetual night,
lit only by starlight. Such is
the fate that lies ahead for the
solar system, in ages beyond
imagining.

SUPERNOVAE AND NEUTRON STARS

The Crab nebula in Taurus is the remnant of a star that exploded into a supernova nearly 1,000 years ago.

Some stars are born with less than a few times the sun's mass and end relatively quietly as white dwarfs. But a more massive star has a more eventful career. During its supergiant stage, its core may suddenly collapse and explode, blowing the whole star to pieces with stupendous violence. A star undergoing this fate is known as a supernova. It shines with a billion or more times the sun's light for several weeks.

Deep within the Crab nebula is a pulsar, which is believed to be the remaining core of the original star. The pulsar's light varies from bright (top) to virtually invisible (bottom).

A star explodes and dies in these two photographs. The photograph (far left) shows the star after it has already exploded. It is now a supernova, many times brighter than the original star. The photograph (near left), taken five years later, shows a cloud of gas in the area, all that remains of the original star.

In the summer of 1054, such an exploding star appeared in the constellation Taurus. For more than three weeks, it was so bright it could be seen in broad daylight, according to the Chinese astronomers who watched it. In the same spot today is the famous Crab nebula, so named because it looked vaguely crablike through telescopes in the 1800's. This nebula is the debris of the stellar explosion that happened over 900 years ago. It is still expanding outward from the explosion site at a speed of several thousand miles per second.

In the center of the Crab nebula is the remainder of the supernova's core. It is an example of the strangest star of all: the pulsar.

Pulsars were first discovered with radio telescopes. In 1967, something in the constellation Vulpecula was found to be emitting regular pulses of radio energy every 1.3 seconds. Nothing known at the time could account for this. The discoverers thought at first they might be picking up signals from another civilization. But pulsars proved to be natural phenomena. Many more were discovered, including the one in the Crab nebula. That one pulses at an especially rapid rate: 30 times a second.

Pulsars are spinning neutron stars. A neutron star is an extremely dense and tiny object, about 10 to 12 miles (16 to 19 kilometers) in diameter. In this small volume is compressed an entire star's mass. A neutron star is rather like a white dwarf carried to ridiculous extremes. The atomic nuclei of its matter are packed very tightly together. Most of them are converted into a fluid of pure neutrons. Hence, a neutron star is mostly liquid, with a solid crust.

The density of a neutron star can be as high as 10 billion tons per cubic inch—hundreds of millions of times greater than even a white dwarf's. Its surface gravity is many billions of times greater than Earth's, surpassing a white dwarf's surface gravity by thousands of times. And the extreme strength of its magnetic field rivals that of its gravity. The conditions on a neutron star are so far beyond human experience that it is almost hopeless to try to imagine them.

137

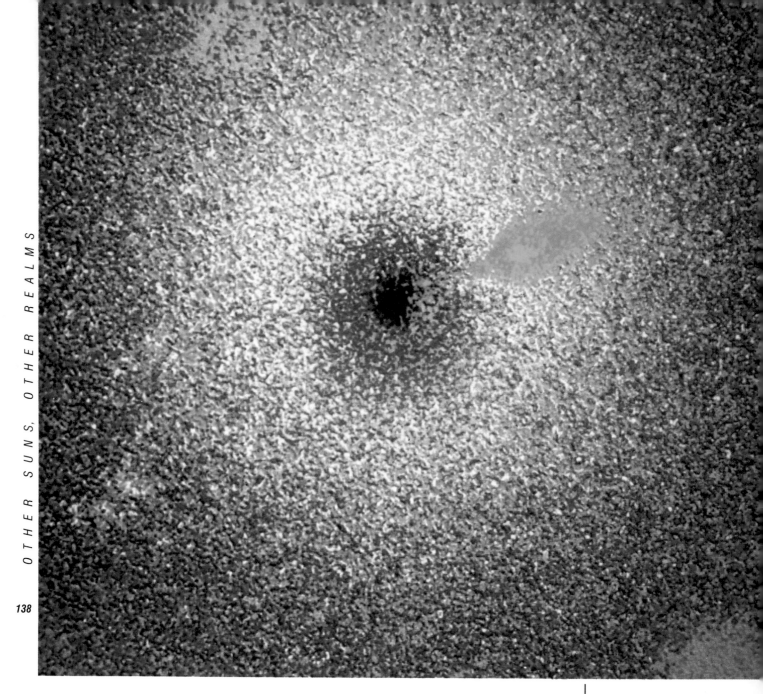

BLACK HOLES

Other than becoming a white dwarf or a neutron star, there is a third possible end to a star's life—a black hole. This is the strangest object of all.

The basic concept of a black hole isn't hard to grasp. Every astronomical body has a certain escape velocity. This is the speed at which an object has to travel in order to escape the body's gravity and enter into space. Earth's escape velocity is 7 miles (11 kilometers) per second. An object traveling upward with less than this speed will fall back down to Earth, while one traveling faster will fly away into space.

The sun's escape velocity is 386 miles (618 kilometers) per second, since the sun is more massive and has stronger gravity

This color-enhanced photograph of the galaxy M87 shows a gas jet shooting out of the galaxy's center. The dark-colored nucleus contains an extremely dense object, presumed to be a black hole.

than Earth. The escape velocity from a neutron star can be as high as 150,000 miles (240,000 kilometers) per second, which is getting close to the speed of light.

What if the escape velocity is greater than the speed of light? Then even a light beam aimed up from the star will curl over and fall back down. No light will escape. To an outside observer, the body would look like a black void.

This much was recognized by astronomers as early as 200 years ago. But the true nature of a black hole had to await Albert Einstein's general theory of relativity. Einstein found that space and time are intimately related, and that gravity consists of a curvature or distortion of four-dimensional space time—something impossible to visualize, but true nonetheless. A black hole is a region with gravity so intense it has removed itself from the rest of space. Nothing is left behind but an opening. With the exception of gamma rays and X rays, nothing ever leaves a black hole. (Like all hot bodies in space, black holes must emit radiation.)

Do such things really exist? The answer is quite possibly yes. If a dead star has a mass greater than about three times the sun's,

it cannot become either a white dwarf or a neutron star. Instead, its gravity is so strong it will keep collapsing indefinitely. As it shrinks, its gravity intensifies, its escape velocity surpasses the speed of light, and it becomes a black hole. From then on, we can see nothing more of it. The hole formed by a star of 10 times the sun's mass will be about 38 miles (61 kilometers) across.

As far as anyone knows, the collapsing star inside might go on shrinking to become a true mathematical point, with zero size and infinite density. Or perhaps at extreme densities, new laws of physics, about which we know nothing, take over. There is reason to think the inside of a rotating black hole may be a gateway to whole other realms of space time and perhaps other universes. However, it is most likely that a human being who either entered or fell into a black hole would be torn apart.

Some black holes may already have been detected. A few double stars have been found in which an invisible member of the pair gives very strong evidence of being a black hole. In addition, much larger black holes with masses of millions or billions of suns might exist at the centers of many galaxies. The question is far from settled, but most astronomers assume the universe does indeed contain black holes in great numbers.

GALAXIES

Arching across the night sky among the stars is a dim, hazy band of light. The Romans called it the *Via Lactea*, meaning the Milky Road or Milky Way. According to one of their legends, it was milk from the goddess Juno. Aside from that, they had no idea what it could be.

Only in the early 1600's, when Galileo turned his telescope on the Milky Way, did its true nature become clear. Its pale glow, Galileo saw, is made up entirely of very faint stars—swarms and

clouds of them "so numerous," he wrote, "as to be almost beyond belief."

Questions immediately arose: Why are so many stars gathered in this narrow band? Why aren't they scattered evenly across the sky?

In the 1700's, English astronomer William Herschel made a

This artist's conception of our Milky Way galaxy shows the spiral arms radiating out from the bright central hub. Our solar system is located in one of these arms.

serious effort to find out. Using his large telescopes, he counted the numbers of faint stars in different places around the sky in hopes of estimating their true distribution in space. He concluded that the universe of stars is arranged in a great, irregular, flat slab, with Earth and the sun deep inside it.

Herschel was not far wrong. Our Milky Way galaxy (the word *galaxy* comes from a Greek word meaning "milk") is indeed a very flat, pancake-shaped swarm of stars with a bulge in the center. We are inside it. We see more stars when we look through its breadth than when we look through its thin sides. This is why the Milky Way seems to ring Earth in a circle. Picture a blueberry's viewpoint inside a pancake; this is similar to our visual perspective of the Milky Way galaxy from Earth.

But the galaxy is much larger than Herschel and other early astronomers thought. They didn't know about interstellar dust that pervades the galaxy and in many places blocks our view beyond a few thousand light-years. Today, we can penetrate through the dust with radio telescopes and other means, and so we have gained a more complete picture of our galaxy.

142

ANATOMY OF THE MILKY WAY

We know our galaxy to be an enormous, flat pinwheel of stars, gas, and dust, indeed about as flat as a pancake. The Milky Way is almost 100,000 light-years across and just a few thousand light-years thick. Its bright central bulge, or nucleus, is somewhat thicker, perhaps 10,000 light-years through.

The sun is located about 30,000 light-years from our galaxy's center, near the inner edge of one of the spiral arms. Most of the stars we see in the sky belong to our small galactic neighborhood. The bright center lies

The Milky Way galaxy, as seen from Earth, is a bright band of stars across the night sky. This photograph shows it to be actually a clustering of stars and dust clouds, strung out unevenly across the night sky.

in the direction of the constellation Sagittarius, and it is hidden from us by dust.

The Milky Way galaxy contains hundreds of billions of stars and extensive clouds of gas and dust. Its spiral arms trail streamers of billions of suns and thousands of bright and dark nebulae. Like all spiral-shaped galaxies, the Milky Way is slowly rotating. The motion is so slow that no change whatever can be seen during the course of human history. The sun, like most of the stars near us, orbits around the galaxy's center once every 250 million years. The

Milky Way has completed perhaps a quarter of a turn in the 65 million years since the dinosaurs died out on Earth.

The galaxy's nucleus is an extraordinary place. Here the stars are much more abundant than in our own thinly populated region in one of the arms. Any planets in the central zone must have skies packed with brilliant stars.

In the center of the nucleus is a mysterious, very small area that emits powerful radio, infrared, and other radiations. It may well involve a massive black hole, whose gravitational energy powers these strange phenomena.

In the outermost parts of the

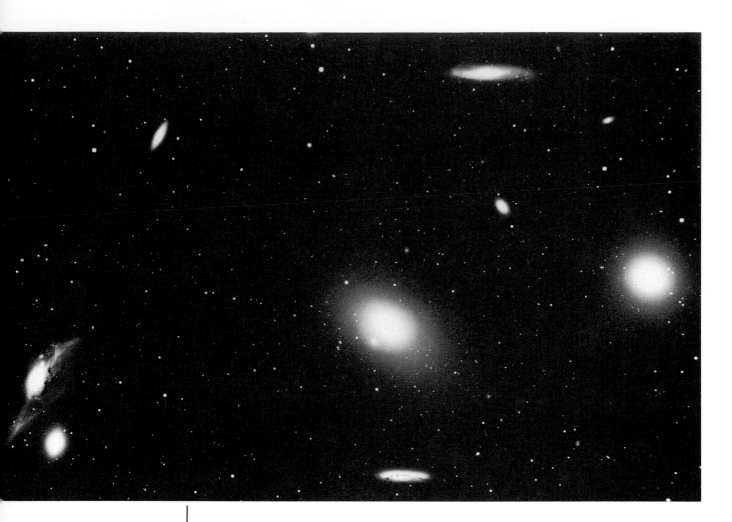

This large cluster of galaxies, located in the constellation Virgo, is about 60 million light-years from the Milky Way galaxy.

galaxy, stars become few and far between. A very large but dim halo of such thinly scattered stars surrounds the Milky Way and other galaxies out to great distances. The halo around the Milky Way is not flat like the disk but is almost spherical. One component of the halo is fairly prominent: the globular clusters, which are dense balls of up to hundreds of thousands of stars. Dozens of globular clusters may be seen with a small telescope, some with a pair of binoculars.

DISCOVERY OF OTHER GALAXIES

The nearest spiral galaxy beyond the Milky Way was long known as the Andromeda nebula. It is a fuzzy patch dimly visible to the naked eye in the evening sky of autumn. In even the best telescopes, it looks like a gaseous, spiral-shaped nebula.

Several thousand other such spiral-shaped nebulae had been cataloged by 1900. Twenty years later, photography was revealing hundreds of thousands of these objects. A debate raged among astronomers about what they are. Some believed the spiral nebulae were just small gas clouds relatively nearby. In this view, the Milky Way was the entire universe. Other astronomers argued that they were whole other Milky Ways extremely far away—separate island universes millions of light-years distant.

By the mid-1920's, the island universe theory was winning. Final proof came when photographs taken with large new telescopes resolved the hazy glow of various nebulae into swarms of extremely faint stars.

We now know that the Andromeda galaxy is 2.2 million light-years away and no longer our closest galactic neighbor. The Magellanic Clouds (so called because they appear cloudy to the naked eye) are galaxies only 160,000 and 180,000 light years away. Other galaxies are much farther away. A large amateur telescope can see certain galaxies as far away as 200 or 300 million light-years.

SPIRALS, ELLIPTICALS, IRREGULARS

Galaxies come in a variety of forms. By the middle of this century, astronomers were photographing them in great numbers and trying to understand their many shapes.

A key discovery made along the way was that there are two kinds of star populations in gal-

Galaxy M51, otherwise known as the Whirlpool galaxy, shows the basic structure of a spiral galaxy.

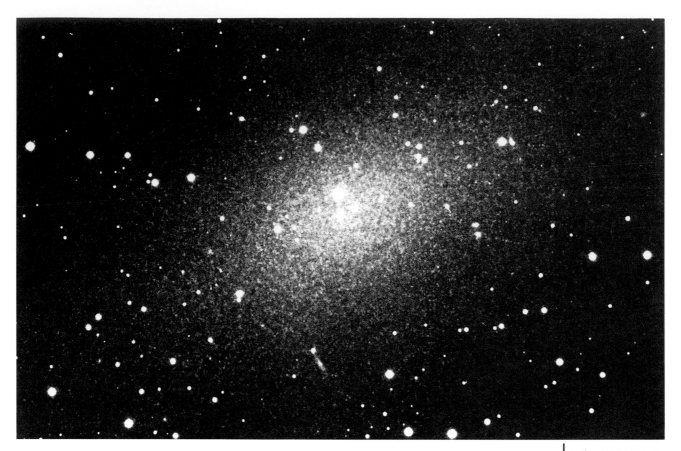

axies. The disks of spiral galaxies contain much gas and dust, as well as many young stars. In these parts of galaxies, including our sun's own region, star formation is still proceeding briskly. The objects making up this part of a galaxy are called Population I objects.

A spiral galaxy's central zone and outer halo are quite different. Here, there is practically no gas and dust. Star formation ceased long ago, and the stars are all very old. These regions contain Population II objects.

Different galaxies have different mixes of the two populations. Some spiral galaxies have very small nuclei, or, in the extreme case of some irregular galaxies, none at all. They are made up almost entirely of Population I material. Other spirals have very big central hubs and almost no spiral arms. Extreme cases are the elliptical galaxies, which are all nucleus: pure Population II material. They have virtually no interstellar matter or young stars at all.

Galaxies were first classified along these lines by Edwin Hubble during the first half of this century. Elliptical, or type E, galaxies lack spiral structure or any detail at all. They are pure hazes of stars. Hubble subdivided the ellipticals into types ranging from E0, for perfect spheres, to E7, for the most elongated ovals.

Spirals, type S, he classified in part by how large the nucleus is compared to the spiral arms. Type S0 is much like an elliptical, having only traces of spiral structure. In type Sa, spiral arms start to be visible; in type Sb the nucleus is smaller and the arms larger; and type Sc has thick, bright arms and a small nucleus.

Galaxy NGC 147 in the constellation Cassiopeia is a good example of an elliptical galaxy. It is a member of the local group to which the Milky Way galaxy also belongs.

The Milky Way is thought to be between type Sb and Sc.

Some spirals have a bar-shaped central hub. These barred spiral galaxies are called SBa, SBb, and SBc.

EVOLUTION OF THE MILKY WAY

The two kinds of star populations are the key to understanding much about the history of the universe. The oldest of Population II stars are almost as old as the universe itself. They are almost pure hydrogen and helium, since that is the material with which the universe began.

All the heavier elements—including most of the atoms making up Earth and our own bodies—were formed later, by nuclear reactions inside the cores of stars. When these stars came to the ends of their lives, they either exploded as supernovae or puffed off their outer layers back into space. Either way, the heavy elements they had created in their cores rejoined the interstellar gas and dust. In this way, the interstellar matter in Population I regions is being slowly enriched with atoms of elements other than hydrogen and helium.

By the time the sun and solar system formed from an interstellar gas cloud, heavy elements had been recycled back into it from earlier generations of stars. So there were enough heavy elements to form planets like Earth.

Everything around us but hydrogen and helium—every rock, tree, bit of metal, even our flesh—is made of atoms that were created inside stars that blew apart billions of years ago. We are made of the ashes of dead suns. The life cycle of the Milky Way galaxy is intimately tied up with the life of our world, and of ourselves.

The Tarantula Nebula is an immense cluster of gas and stars on the southeastern edge of the Large Magellanic Cloud. The center (lower left) gives off 50 million times as much energy as our sun.

147

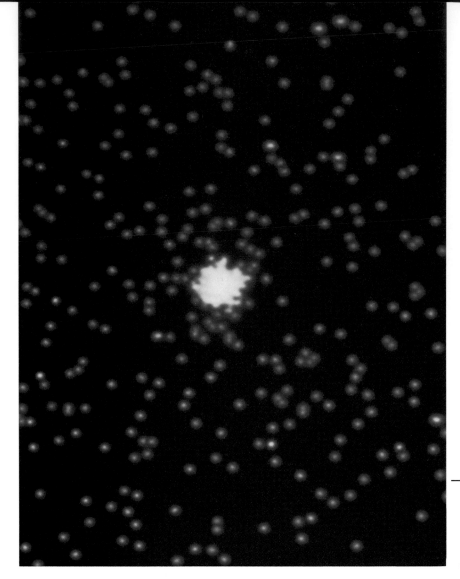

QUASARS

Throughout this book, we have been looking farther and farther out into space. Let's speed up the journey and extend our view to the very limits of the observable universe.

As far as can be seen in any direction beyond the Milky Way, space is sprinkled with other galaxies. They usually group together in what are known as galaxy clusters. Our Milky Way is itself part of a small cluster known as the Local Group; it is a few million light-years across.

As we look farther out to tens and hundreds of millions of light-years, the clusters themselves gather into superclusters.

Our Local Group is on the edge of the nearest supercluster, whose center is in the constellation Virgo at a distance of 30 or 40 million light-years.

The farther we look into the distance, the smaller and fainter galaxies appear. At several billion light-years, they have shrunk almost to pinpoints, barely distinguishable from faint foreground stars in the best telescopes. Yet, even at this tremendous distance, galaxies all seem to be pretty much alike. All other parts of the known universe appear to be just about the same as our own region.

ACTIVE GALACTIC NUCLEI

Beyond a billion light-years or so, however, a new and very rare type of object starts appearing. In

Many astronomers believe only one known source of energy can produce so much light: matter falling into a very massive black hole. As material nears the black hole's edge, it becomes extremely compressed and heated and can give off more energy than even nuclear reactions could provide. A quasar is thought by some to be powered by a black hole weighing millions or billions of solar masses, located at a normal galaxy's core. We don't see the rest of this galaxy because the quasar so greatly outshines it.

In fact, weaker objects of the same kind are found in the cores of certain galaxies nearby. These active galactic nuclei are like miniature quasars. Even the Milky Way seems to have a black hole at its center, emitting still less energy—presumably because less matter is falling into it.

Still, much remains to be learned about quasars. Some astronomers believe that they are not nearly as far away as the edge of the universe, but their evidence is not strong. More powerful telescopes and other technological advances should help us learn much more about these mysterious objects in the years to come.

the early 1960's, astronomers started finding brilliant, starlike objects at these distances that were putting out so much light they defied all reason. They were given the name quasi-stellar objects, or quasars. A quasar is many times more brilliant than an entire galaxy with hundreds of billions of suns. The record-holding quasar as of 1985 is 100,000 times more luminous than the entire Milky Way.

Yet, these objects must be much smaller than galaxies. They have been seen to vary in brightness, and in radio and X-ray output, as rapidly as in a few weeks or days. This must mean they are no larger than a few light-weeks or light-days in size. Otherwise, variations at different parts of the quasar would cancel out, and we would not see any changes. By comparison, recall that a galaxy is typically 100,000 light-years in size. For all its brilliance, a quasar is not much larger than the solar system.

In 1963, Quasar 3C 273 became the first quasar to be identified optically.

THE CREATION OF
THE UNIVERSE

Galaxies drift apart

Galaxies and stars

Matter

Primordial fireball

Big bang

Time zero

Have you ever heard a car driving past you with its horn blowing steadily? If so, you may have noticed something strange. As the car approached, the horn was high-pitched, but it dropped to a lower pitch as soon as it went by.

The horn itself didn't change. The driver of the car heard the same pitch all along, even while you heard it sliding down to a lower note. What you heard was an everyday example of what is known as the Doppler effect. Astronomers have turned this phenomenon into one of their most useful tools.

As the car is approaching, sound waves from the horn pile up in front of it. Thus the distance between each wave—the wavelength—becomes shorter, corresponding to a higher pitch. As the car recedes, the sound waves are spread farther out behind it, so the wavelength is longer and the pitch is lower.

The same effect occurs with light waves. A star approaching us has its light shortened in wavelength. This is called blue-shifting light because blue light

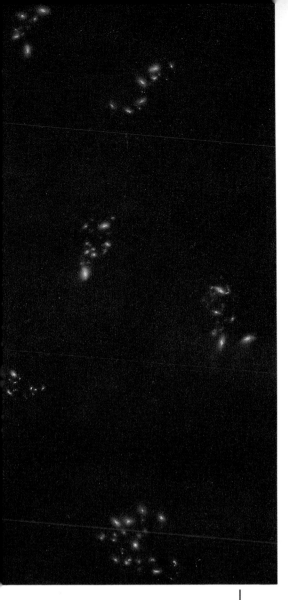

This is a "picture" of the history and future of the universe according to the big bang theory. At time zero, all forces and matter were unified. There was no time or space. The big bang was triggered and the universe was born, consisting chiefly of strong radiation, pure energy. Within a fraction of a second, the universe became a rapidly expanding primordial fireball. Atomic nuclei began forming. After a few hundred years, the still-expanding fireball consisted mostly of matter, mainly in the form of hydrogen and some helium. After about 100 million years, matter started forming into galaxies and stars. As the universe continually expanded, the galaxies also drifted apart, moving farther and farther away from each other. The universe will continue expanding forever, the galaxies moving ever farther apart.

has the shortest waves. A receding star has its light red-shifted to longer wavelengths. By measuring the wavelengths of a star's spectral lines, its velocity toward or away from us can be found with great precision.

THE BIG BANG

In the early 1900's, astronomers began measuring the velocities of galaxies by this method. By 1929, a very strange fact was showing up. Distant galaxies are all moving away from us. The light coming from them is redshifted. The farther a galaxy is, the faster it is fleeing away.

At first, it might seem like the Milky Way exerts some kind of repulsive power that pushes other galaxies off. But astronomers quickly realized that the situation would look just the same from anywhere else in the universe. Every galaxy, disregarding small local motions, is moving away from every other.

Imagine a balloon with dots painted on it. As the balloon is blown up, every dot gets farther from its neighbors. The galaxies are like the dots. Space itself, like the balloon, is enlarging and carrying them apart.

If the galaxies are all flying apart, then obviously they were closer together in the past. Tracing back the paths of the fleeing galaxies, astronomers realized that they all—indeed, all the matter in the universe—were packed together in a dense mass 10 to 20 billion years ago.

The universe is expanding like the debris of a gigantic explosion. Astronomers named this event the big bang. It was an amazing discovery and completely unexpected. Some astronomers resisted the idea of a big bang and looked for ways the ex-

pansion of the universe could happen without it. They invented steady state theories allowing the universe to be infinitely old. But most astronomers abandoned these theories.

Strong proof for the big bang theory came in 1965 when two scientists working for Bell Laboratories were testing a sensitive microwave antenna. Microwaves are short radio waves. From all parts of the sky, the antenna picked up weak but unexplained microwave noise. This microwave background radiation is thought to have come from the big bang fireball itself. It is probably the actual white light of the big bang explosion, red-shifted all the way down into the microwave spectrum during its 10 to 20-billion-year flight through the expanding universe.

THE FIRST MOMENTS OF EXISTENCE

The study of the universe as a whole is called cosmology. In recent years, a key part of cosmology has consisted of following the big bang back to earlier and earlier moments, ever closer to what is called time zero. Let's follow this hypothetical trail of events.

The microwave background radiation is believed to have come from the big bang fireball as it stood when the universe was only about 700,000 years old. The farther back we look, the hotter and denser the universe becomes. When the universe was only a few minutes old, scientists believe it was hot enough for nuclear reactions to fuse hydrogen into helium. The ratio of helium to hydrogen we see in the cosmos today is evidence of events that may have taken place only a few minutes from time zero.

We can follow the big bang still further back, again, hypothetically. At the first ten-thousandth of a second, the tempera-

151

Steady state theory

Big bang theory

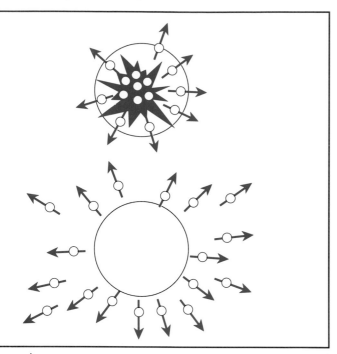

The steady state theory claims that the universe has always been expanding at a constant rate and that new matter is constantly being created (top). Hence, there is always the same amount of matter in a given space (bottom).

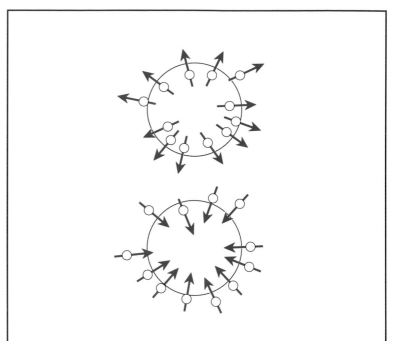

The big bang theory states that the universe began with a huge explosion (top) and that all galaxies will expand and move away from the center of the universe indefinitely (bottom).

152

ture of the universe was about 1.8 trillion degrees Fahrenheit (1 trillion degrees Celsius). Everything would have been a pure, uniform sea of radiation and elementary particles, mostly protons, neutrons, and electrons.

A similar situation prevailed at still earlier times and higher temperatures. Going even further back, physicists now believe that tremendously important events took place at the incredible time of 10^{-35} second after time zero. Written out, this fraction of a second would be a decimal point followed by 34 zeros and a 1. Before this time, the universe may have been hot enough to unite all the basic forces of nature except gravity into one grand unified force. The separation of these forces at this time may have given rise to the laws of physics that govern the universe now.

The going gets even more difficult here. But physicists have been tremendously excited in recent years by the way many features of the modern universe are explained by events at this incredibly early moment. The scenarios involved are called inflationary universe theories, because they require the big bang to go through very sudden enlargement, or inflation, at this time.

It may seem incredible that we can actually know what happened in such a brief moment so long ago. But, if the inflationary universe theories hold up, events at that time made the kind of universe we have today. We may thus be surrounded by evidence of what happened in the very first instant of the big bang.

THE MOMENT OF CREATION

What caused the big bang? Where did it come from? Until recently, no one had the slightest idea. Time zero seemed to be where science came to a halt. Yet, buried in the laws of atomic behavior that govern the everyday world, an answer may be hidden. There are certain cir-

Pulsating universe theory

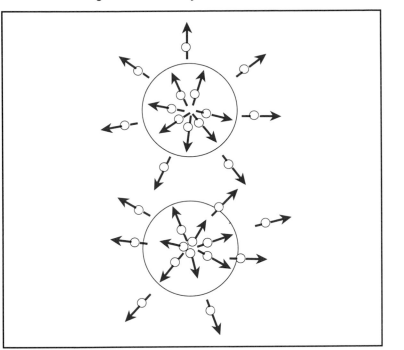

The pulsating universe theory states that all galaxies are flying apart from a previously compacted mass (top). This expansion will eventually stop, and the universe will begin to contract, due to gravity (bottom). When the universe becomes highly condensed, it will explode and begin another phase of expansion.

cumstances under which a particle of matter—an electron, say—appears out of absolutely nothing, exists for a brief instant, and vanishes back into nothing. This is seen happening in laboratory settings all the time.

The theory describing these events, if applied to the universe, would allow for larger masses to be spontaneously created out of absolute nothingness in the same way. Once this happens, the inflationary universe process can take over and cause a full-blown big bang.

MANY UNIVERSES

And there's more. All such theories predict that if a big bang can happen once, it can happen many times. There may be many other universes, resulting from many other big bangs. It is no use to ask where these other universes are. They are completely separate from our universe, our bubble of space time. If they do exist, they would probably be in some sort of different dimension we cannot break into. So how can we ever find out if other universes really exist? Perhaps we will never know.

Then again, some scientists think a piece of evidence is already at hand. There are many strange coincidences in the laws of physics governing our universe, and these coincidences are very lucky for us as living beings. No life of any kind could exist if certain physical laws were changed by a tiny amount.

It looks as if the universe were carefully hand-adjusted to allow the existence of living things.

On the other hand, these strange coincidences may be accounted for if there are indeed many universes, as these newest big bang theories predict. Most universes would lack the special coincidences allowing life. So they would remain forever barren. Only a very few may happen, purely by chance, to have the right conditions. Therefore, we might be in one of the rare universes that allows life. So even though it looks specially fine-tuned, our universe may have come about as much by chance as all the others.

THE FRONTIERS OF KNOWLEDGE

In the last few centuries, we have gone from thinking that Earth is the center of the universe to understanding that it goes around the sun; from seeing the sun as the center of everything to recognizing that it is just one star lost among the swarms of stars in the Milky Way; from thinking the Milky Way is the only galaxy to recognizing that there are many others. And now, we may be on the edge of seeing our universe, the result of our big bang, as itself being only one of many.

The realms outside and before the big bang must be the wildest, least known, and most exciting frontiers of science. Untold discoveries are just beginning to open up, and realms of which we have no conception may be explored in the lifetimes of people now living.

153

Index

Acknowledgments

The publishers acknowledge the following sources for illustrations. Credits read from top to bottom, left to right, on their respective pages. Charts and diagrams prepared by the WORLD BOOK staff unless otherwise noted.

Cover Jet Propulsion Laboratory (JPL).
8 Gary Ladd; The British Museum.
9 WORLD BOOK photo. **10** Anthony Miles, Bruce Coleman Inc. **12** The Metropolitan Museum of Art, New York.
14–16 Granger Collection. **17** Granger Collection; Bettmann Archive.
18–19 Granger Collection. **20** National Portrait Gallery, London; Culver Pictures. **21** Dennis Di Cicco. **24** High Altitude Observatory, National Center for Atmospheric Research; National Aeronautics and Space Administration (NASA); JPL. **25** National Optical Astronomy Observatories (NOAO); NASA. **26** NASA. **30** C. Falco, Photo Researchers. **31** Kitt Peak National Observatory. **32** High Altitude Observatory; Ned Haines, Photo Researchers. **34** Rob Wood, Stansbury, Ronsaville, Wood, Inc. **38** Anne Norcia. **40** NASA. **48** Mount Wilson and Palomar Observatories. **49** Bettmann Archive. **51** NASA. **52** Russ Kinne, Photo Researchers. **53** JPL. **54** Dennis Di Cicco. **56** TASS from Sovfoto. **58** JPL. **59** JPL; Lowell Observatory. **60** NASA. **63** JPL. **64** JPL; NASA; Lowell Observatory. **66** JPL. **68** Kinuko Craft. **69** American Museum of Natural History. **71** Ernest Chilson, Flagstaff Chamber of Commerce; James M. Baker. **72–80** JPL. **82** NASA. **84** William K. Hartmann; Bettmann Archive. **85** NASA; JPL. **86** Roberta Polfus. **87–92** JPL. **93** Lunar and Planetary Laboratory, University of Arizona, NASA. **94** Don Dixon; G. P. Kuiper, Yerkes Observatory. **96** Don Dixon; U.S. Naval Observatory. **97** Hale Observatories. **98** C. Nicollier. **100** WORLD BOOK files; Rob Wood, Stansbury, Ronsaville, Wood, Inc. **102** James Sugar, Black Star; U.S. Naval Observatory; NOAO. **103** Jean Lorre, Science Photo Library. **104** Simone D. Gossner, Smithsonian Institution. **106–107** WORLD BOOK illustrations by W. J. M. Tirion. **108** Roberta Polfus. **111** Anne Norcia. **112** U.S. Naval Observatory. **116** Glenn Gustafson. **118** Ray Villard, Davis Planetarium. **121** Bettmann Archive. **122** © Royal Observatory Edinburgh (David F. Malin, Anglo-Australian Observatory). **124** © Royal Observatory Edinburgh (David F. Malin, Anglo-Australian Observatory); Lick Observatory. **125** Roberta Polfus. **126** George East. **130** California Institute of Technology. **132** Roberta Polfus. **134** WORLD BOOK illustration by Herb Herrick. **136** California Institute of Technology and Carnegie Institution of Washington; Lick Observatory. **137** Hale Observatories. **138** Jean Lorre, Science Photo Library. **140** WORLD BOOK illustration by Anne Norcia. **142** Lund Observatory, Sweden. **144** Kitt Peak National Observatory. **145** Science Photo Library. **146** Hale Observatories. **147** David Malin and Ray Sharples, Anglo-Australian Telescope Board. **148** H. Tananbaum, Harvard/ Smithsonian Center for Astrophysics, Cambridge, MA. **149** NOAO. **150** Don Dixon.

World Book Encyclopedia, Inc. offers a wide range of educational and reference materials, including a video—"How to Study." This 45-minute VHS tape combines the appeal of television with an easy-to-use formula for developing successful study habits. For more information on World Book's "How to Study" video, as well as our wide selection of educational and reference books, please write:
World Book Encyclopedia, Inc.
P.O. Box 3405, Chicago, Illinois 60654-9980.